Classic Quilts in a Day

Fran Roen

STERLING PUBLISHING CO., INC.
NEW YORK

This book is dedicated to the one who has always been there for me in times of joy and sorrow, my best friend, Jah, as well as to my family: my husband, Ron; my children Cressenda, Carry, Caleb, Charlyn, Clint, and Charlie. They are wonderful!

Library of Congress Cataloging-in-Publication Data

Roen, Fran.
    Classic quilts in a day / by Fran Roen.
      p. cm.
    Includes index.
    ISBN 0-8069-0758-4
    1. Quilting—Patterns. 2. Quilts—United States—History.
  I. Title.
    TT835.R6248 1994
    746.46—dc20   94-26051
                                          CIP

Photography by Nancy Palubniak

Illustrations by Fran Roen

Edited by Isabel Stein

10 9 8 7 6 5 4 3 2 1

Published by Sterling Publishing Company, Inc.
387 Park Avenue South, New York, N.Y. 10016
© 1994 by Fran Roen
Distributed in Canada by Sterling Publishing
% Canadian Manda Group, One Atlantic Avenue, Suite 105
Toronto, Ontario, Canada M6K 3E7
Distributed in Great Britain and Europe by Cassell PLC
Villiers House, 41/47 Strand, London WC2N 5JE, England
Distributed in Australia by Capricorn Link (Australia) Pty Ltd.
P.O. Box 6651, Baulkham Hills, Business Centre, NSW 2153, Australia
Manufactured in the United States of America
All rights reserved

Sterling ISBN 0-8069-0758-4

Contents

Fan Quilt (see page 23)

Materials, Tools, and Other Basics

BACKING

The backing is the underside or bottom of your quilt—usually it is made with 6 or 7 yards of 100% cotton fabric. Some people like to use sheets for the back. If you decide to do this, remove all selvedges and seams, and wash the sheet to remove the sizing. Always buy a sheet one size larger than the quilt you're making. Most sheets are made of percale, which is a very tight weave. Don't use this if you plan to hand-quilt your project; it's very hard to push a needle through it.

BATTING

Batting is the filling that goes between your pieced quilt top and the backing. As a rule there are three fibers or combinations of fibers that are used in batting: cotton, cotton/polyester, and polyester. Cotton is flat and is only about ¾-inch thick. It's nice because it's cool in the summer and hot in the winter, because it absorbs moisture. Cotton/polyester blend is from 2 to 4 inches in thickness (loft). It is nice to work with, as it is a blend of the best qualities of cotton and polyester: it's warm and lofty without a lot of weight. Also, it's cool in the summer. Polyester can be up to 6 inches thick, so it can be really puffed up. One of the nice things about polyester is that it is mildew-resistant; you can buy it bonded, which is perfect for tied quilts. It's also moth-resistant, warm, and nonallergenic.

While we're talking about batting, we should also mention loft (thickness). There is low-loft, which is about ½-inch thick, medium loft, about ¾ to 1 inch thick, and high loft, which is about 1 to 2 inches thick. Finally, there is extra high-loft, about 2 to 4 inches thick.

Have you ever taken your polyester batting out of its plastic bag and then tried to get it back in? It won't go, will it? That's because as soon as you take it out of the bag, the batting begins to fill with air: this is called *breathing*. When you open the bag, you'll notice that there may appear to be both thin and clumpy areas. What you need to do is lay the batting out open on a table overnight to allow the batting to breathe. If you don't have the space or time to do this, put the batting in the dryer on the delicate cycle for a few minutes.

CHOOSING COLORS

There are many ways of choosing color harmonies. I choose a large printed piece of fabric that I really like and build from it. Then I pick out colors from the large print to use in the rest of the quilt. Even if I don't actually use the large print in the quilt, I know that the colors go together. It's wise to be careful when using large prints in quilts, since more than one large print in a quilt may make it appear too busy. Large prints may work well in large areas.

Whatever colors you choose to use, remember to consider the dark and light contrast. For example, if you want the points of a star to show up, you may choose dark points with a light background. Medium colors against medium colors will blend and therefore will not stand out.

Flowers, or a favorite painting, rug, or piece of pottery may also serve as sources of color combinations; see also the Color Harmony Table (at back of book).

It's very helpful to get some graph paper and colored pencils and do some color sketches of color combinations you are considering. Where construction diagrams are given, you can photocopy them and color them in. In addition to helping you choose a color combination, your colored sketch can serve as a guide to shopping for fabric, piecing, and assembly later on.

FABRIC

Using 100% cotton makes for a nice quilt; however, you can use many other fabrics for quilting, as long as your choices all have the same weight and fabric content. Some fabrics, like polyester, tend to hold stains, however, and should be avoided.

All fabrics should be prewashed. Check to make sure all your fabrics are colorfast when you wash them. If you find you have a "bleeder," one whose dye isn't permanently set, fill your washing machine to its lowest level with cold water and add a mixture of 1¼ cups of white vinegar and ½ cup of salt; this mixture will set the colors nicely. The fabric should soak for at least four hours; overnight, when possible, is better. If the fabric still bleeds after this, then label your finished quilt "dry clean only," or simply choose a different fabric if you want a washable quilt.

FUSIBLE INTERFACING

Fusible interfacing is suggested for machine appliqué work in this book. The interfacing is used to adhere small pieces of cloth (the appliqués) to background fabric. This will allow both your hands to remain free during the stitching phase. The heat of an iron fuses the interfacing to the fabric, so follow the instructions of the particular manufacturer as to how hot to set your iron for proper adherence and for other details. Not all interfacing is 45 inches wide, so try to estimate what area of interfacing you will need for a project and adjust the yardage as necessary if it is narrower. There are many brands and weights of fusible interfacing; there is even double-sided interfacing, with adhesive on both sides. The projects in this book use interfacing that has adhesive on one side. One deciding factor in planning the projects this way was expense; the double-sided interfacing is more expensive. You don't have to use fusible interfacing at all; you can add ⅛ inch all the way around to the appliqué templates that have been provided and fold under a ¼-inch hem, pin the appliqué in place, and stitch it to the background fabric. But the fusible interfacing *is* a time-saver.

IRON

Pressing is a must. When pressed, your blocks will be kept flat, without puckers or unwanted folds. Pressing also helps to keep the blocks square. Remember, there is a difference between pressing and ironing. Pressing is, just as the word implies, pressing the weight of the iron down on your fabric to achieve an even heat flow.

Ironing is done with a back-and-forth movement of the iron. Ironing may cause the small pieces of fabric used in quilting to roll or stretch out of shape.

NEEDLES AND HOOP

Always keep a good supply of needles on hand. If your sewing machine needle is bent or rough, replace it. Don't wait until it breaks. Sewing machine needles sizes 12 and 14 work well for machine quilting. For hand quilting, "betweens," sized 7 to 12, work best. Use quilting thread for hand quilting if possible. For tying your quilts, you will need a large-eyed needle to use with a good-quality yarn or embroidery floss. If you hand-quilt, you will need a quilting hoop or frame to hold your work while you quilt. If you are using a hoop and you will be putting your work down for any length of time, remember to remove the hoop to prevent marks or creasing.

PRESSING SURFACE

Use an ironing board or an ironing pad. To make your own ironing pad, buy an ironing board cover. Measure about 2 feet up from the bottom of the cover, and cut it across. Remove all elastic and square off the cover. Cut a piece of batting and backing the same size, and sew all three layers together. Cover up the raw edges with bias tape. Now you can press anywhere without worrying about damaging the surface that's beneath the pad.

QUILTING PINS

Extra-long quilting pins are the most practical type to use for these projects. Have a number of large safety pins on hand also, if you plan to hand- or machine-quilt your projects. Safety pins are used for pin basting, an alternative to thread basting. It will take about 20 to 24 dozen pins to piece together a king-size quilt.

ROTARY CUTTER AND MAT

After the sewing machine, a rotary cutter and mat are the most important aids to speed quilting. Rotary cutters are generally sold in two sizes: small and large. The choice is a matter of personal preference. There are many sizes of mats. You absolutely need a mat if you're using a rotary cutter. Without a mat or cutting board under your fabric, your work surface will become badly scored and your cutter blade will quickly dull. Rotary cutters are very sharp. Be sure to keep them out of the reach of small children, and keep the blade covered when not in use.

RULER

Because most patterns in this book require 2½-inch-wide strips, I went to my local hardware store and had them cut a piece of Plexiglas plastic that measures 2½ inches by 27 inches to use as a guide. (If you do this, make sure that the plastic measures 2½ inches all the way down. I had one once that was 2½ inches at the top, but at the bottom it measured 1¾ inches.) The best thing to use for quiltmaking is an acrylic quilter's ruler, but these can be expensive. Plexiglas is a very affordable alternative.

SEAM RIPPER

A seam ripper is a hooklike blade for ripping seams. We are all imperfect; this tool allows us to get rid of our mistakes quickly and cleanly. Mine is always nearby.

SCISSORS

It's a good idea to keep a pair of sharp scissors next to your sewing machine. That way, you can cut off small threads right away instead of having to go back and cut them later. Also keep a pair on your worktable. This will help to avoid running back and forth to the sewing machine for a pair of scissors.

THREAD

Cotton thread is best, but it is often hard to come by. Cotton-covered polyester thread is much more readily available and works well. I really like cone thread, available for sergers; if your sewing machine doesn't have a setup for it, you can buy an adapter. But whatever you choose, remember that you want your quilt to last, so select the best quality thread that you can afford.

SEWING MACHINE

Any well-running sewing machine will do. If you have a serger, I would suggest using it, but you can get along just fine without one. Make sure that your sewing machine is well-oiled, that the thread tension is on the correct setting, and that it's clean. Nothing seems to stop a project as fast as a poorly operating sewing machine. Unfortunately, most of those stopped projects never seem to get finished. For machine quilting, a walking foot or darning foot are helpful additions.

Now that we have the materials and tools needed to make a quilt, let's see if we can cut some time off the production of our quilt. That will be covered in the next chapter, "Speed Techniques."

Speed Techniques

USING A ROTARY CUTTER

Cutting Strips

Lay your rotary cutting mat on your work surface. Then lay down your first piece of fabric so that the grain is vertical to you (selvages at top and bottom of cutting board). Now lay down any other equal-sized fabric that needs to be cut to the same size over it so they are one on top of the other, with all grains aligned in the same direction. Make sure all layers of the fabrics are smooth. All strips will be cut with the grain, from selvage to selvage.

Before cutting your first strip, even off the edges so that they all line up and are squared up. Then, using your ruler, measure the needed number of inches in from the fabric's edge, press down firmly on your ruler, and run your rotary cutter along the ruler's edge. If you did not cut through all layers, go back with your scissors and finish. As you become more experienced, you will learn to apply just the right amount of pressure to avoid this problem. If your fabric is too wide to fit on your cutting board, you can fold it up from selvedge to selvedge and cut through both layers at once.

The rotary cutter can cut through as many as six layers of fabric at one time. Remember that the more fabric you cut at one time, the greater the pressure you'll need to apply to the cutter. (A helpful hint: the more vertical the rotary cutter, the less pressure you'll need.) If you are right-handed, place all your fabric to the right (see illu. 1). Then start cutting strips at the far left, from the top down the length of your ruler. Move to the right for your next cut. If you are left-handed, do the opposite.

Don't include the selvages in your strips. Trim them off, as they have a tighter weave than the rest of the fabric and are very hard to hand-quilt through.

CHAIN PIECING

Choose a pair of strips you need to join. With right sides of fabric together, sew the length of the strips along one side without cutting them loose from the sewing machine when you come to the end. Next, simply butt in the next set of strips (see illu. 2), and continue sewing. Continue joining the other pairs of strips until you have sewn all of them together. After you finish sewing, you can simply cut the thread between the strip units to divide them up. This is a real time-saver. Chain piecing can be done for joining triangles, squares, or any other units that repeat as well.

HALF-SQUARE TRIANGLES AND TRIANGLE SQUARES

A half-square triangle is one-half of a square pieced from two triangles of different fabrics (illu. 3). The square itself is referred to as a *triangle square*. Speed piecing enables you to make many at once, as described below.

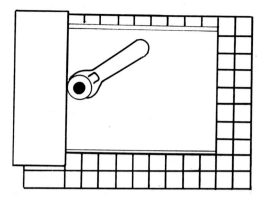

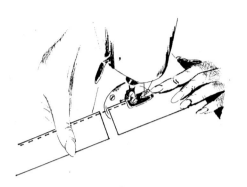

1. *Cutting strips with a rotary cutter.*

2. *Chain piecing.*

3. *A triangle square.*

For the first method (the one that will be used in this book), take two equal-sized rectangles of the two fabrics you want in your triangle squares. Draw a grid of squares on the wrong side of the darker fabric with a light-colored pencil or tailor's chalk, dividing it up into squares (illu. 4). (You could also use a darker pencil on light-colored fabric.) If your finished square (without seam allowances) is supposed to measure 4 inches, for example, your grid should consist of 4⅞-inch squares. (You will lose the seam allowances and later on will lose another ½ inch in seam allowances when the square is joined to the rest of the quilt top.) After you have drawn the grid, draw a diagonal line through each of the squares (see illu. 4).

Next, lay your marked fabric face down on the face-up piece of fabric you wish to join to it. Pin the two together with right sides of fabric facing. Now you are ready to sew the triangles. Line up the fabric on your sewing machine so that the needle is ¼ inch away from the first solid diagonal line, and sew piecing lines following the length of the ruled line, but ¼-inch away from it. Make sure that you pick up the needle each time you come to the point of another triangle (see illu. 4). Do not sew through it. When you have finished the first line, lift up your needle, turn your fabric 180°, and sew along the other side of the first diagonal line, making sure to leave a ¼-seam allowance as before. When you have sewn along both sides of all the diagonal lines, cut along the ruled lines of the squares and along the diagonal ruled lines. Your triangle squares are now ready to be opened up and pressed, and used in your quilt top as necessary.

The second method: Another way to make a triangle square is to cut two bias strips, one out of each of the fabrics you want to join for the triangle squares. If your completed square (without seam allowances) is to be 4 inches × 4 inches, cut out strips 3½ inches wide. With right sides of fabric facing, sew the strips on both long sides with a ¼-inch seam allowance. Next, cut a 4⅞ inch × 4⅞ square of cardboard, mark its diagonal, and cut it on the diagonal. Now you have two templates. To cut out your squares, place the long side of your template flush with the raw edge of the long side of the strip, trace around the template, and cut out a triangle through both thicknesses of fabric (illu. 5). Flip the triangle over so its long side is on the other raw edge, and cut another triangle square.

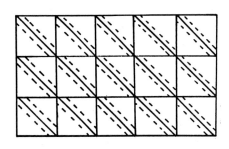

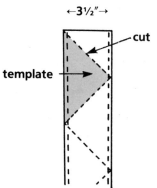

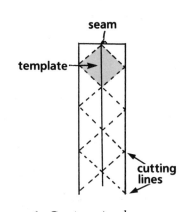

4. Diagram for speed piecing triangle squares (Method 1). Dashed lines are sewing lines; solid lines are cutting lines.

5. Cutting triangle squares, Method 2.

6. Cutting triangle squares, Method 3.

Third method: For the third way of making triangle squares, cut two bias strips of the fabrics you want to join, 3½ inches wide each (for 4-inch finished squares). Then sew the length of your strips together, with right sides of fabric facing, on one long side only. Press the strips open, with the seam allowance toward the darker fabric. Cut a 4½-inch × 4½ inch square of cardboard, mark its diagonal, and use the square as a template. Align the diagonal of the template on the seamline as shown in illu. 6, trace around it, and cut out the square.

QUARTER-SQUARE TRIANGLES

A quarter-square triangle is one quarter of a square. When you put 4 of them together on their bias edges, you have a 4-triangle square (illu. 7). They could be made of four different fabrics; in this book, they are used in the Ohio Star pattern and are made of only two different fabrics. The quick-piecing method of making them makes them easy and fast to do. Take two equal-sized rectangles of the two fabrics for the triangles. Following similar instructions to Method 1 for making 2-triangle squares, rule squares on the wrong side of the lighter fabric. The squares should be 1⅜" larger on a side than the finished size of the 4-triangle square (measured without seam allowances). For example, if the finished square is to be 4 inches × 4 inches, rule squares 5⅜ inches × 5⅜ inches. Rule diagonals on the square grid and seam the two fabrics ¼ inch away from the diagonals, as you did for Method 1 of the triangle square (see illu. 8). Cut your squares apart through

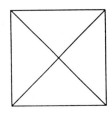

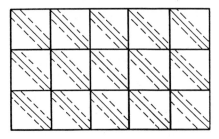

7. A 4-triangle square.

8. For 4-triangle squares, first cut apart on the square lines only (heavy solid lines).

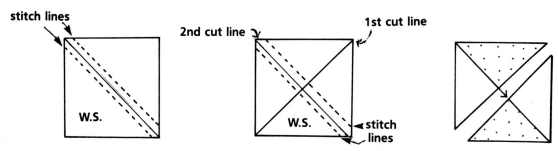

9. A square unit cut out of the grid (4-triangle squares).

10. Marking the first cut line for 4-triangle squares.

11. Joining two pieced triangles to make a 4-triangle square.

both layers of fabric, as shown in illu. 8. Your units will look like illu. 9. Mark the opposite diagonal (illu. 10) and cut the square units in half on that diagonal through both layers of fabric. Then cut on the diagonal cut lines between the stitch lines (2nd cut line). When they are opened out, you will have 4 pieced triangles from each square. Stitch two pieced triangles together as shown in illu. 11, with right sides of fabric facing and ¼″ seam allowances. Press open to form the 4-triangle square. A word of caution: Watch where your fabrics fall if they have patterns, so that you achieve the desired results.

SPEED APPLIQUÉ

This is a wonderful appliqué method if you hate to work around raw edges and pins, as I do. Lay down the fusible interfacing with the adhesive side face up. Top it with your fabric, face down. Cut out your reversed appliqué pattern shape from both layers. Stitch within ¼ inch of the reversed edge, all the way around, through both the fabric and interfacing. Clip any curved edges. Carefully cut an X in the interfacing only. Pull the fabric through the hole, and smooth out the edges.

You now have the right side of the fabric on the top, with the glue side of the interfacing on the bottom. Lay the appliqué in place on the background fabric, and apply it with a warm iron. It will now stay in place for you to stitch around. No pins, no sliding, and no raw edges. There is a transparent nylon thread on the market that allows you to stitch without having the top stitching show; it can be used for stitching the appliqué to the background. Or you may choose thread the same color as your appliqué fabric, or a contrasting color.

ADDING BORDERS

The Basic Idea

In this book, all the quilt patterns have Amish (unmitred) borders, and many patterns suggest using three borders. To adjust the size of your quilt, you may wish to add or subtract borders, however. The borders are pieced by joining 45-inch-wide pieces (cut across the width of the fabric), which reduces the amount of yardage you would otherwise have to buy to make an unpieced border.

Here is an example of border requirements for one quilt and how to make the borders (illu. 12):

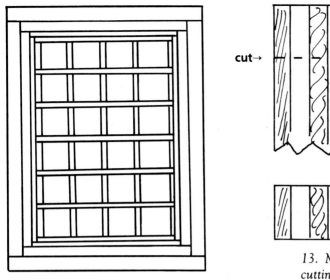

12. Diagram of quilt showing 3 borders.

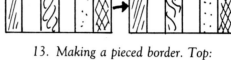

13. Making a pieced border. Top: cutting the strips. Bottom: joining the strip units.

Inner border: eight strips, each 3 × 45 inches
Middle border: eight strips, each 4 × 45 inches
Outer border: eight strips, each 5 × 45 inches

For the inner border, take two 3 × 45-inch strips and sew the two together on a short side. Repeat this a total of four times. Pin the border to the side of the pieced quilt center, with right sides of fabric facing. The length of the inner side border should be the same length as the side of the quilt center. Trim off any excess length of border fabric and sew the border to the quilt center, with ¼-inch seam allowances. (All piecing in the book is to be done with ¼-inch seam allowances, unless otherwise noted.) The top and bottom inner borders need to extend the width of the quilt center *plus* the side inner borders' widths. Pin, trim, and sew the top and bottom inner borders to the quilt top and bottom in the same way that the side borders were attached. The middle and outer borders are pinned, measured, and attached in the same way as the inner border (illu. 12).

Pieced Borders
Pieced borders can add character to a quilt and are very easy to make. See the Fan Quilt (Project 1) for an example of a pieced border. To make a pieced border, make strips of colors that you want to be in the border. Sew them together lengthwise in a pleasing order so you have a pieced sheet of cloth. Then measure down lengthwise from the top of the sheet and cut across all the strips at once (illu. 13). Continue to cut your sheet into pieces of equal length. Sew the cut pieces together on their sides, in repeating order, to form a pieced border. The pieced border then may be sewn to the quilt top in the same way as any other border.

MARKING THE QUILT TOP
Some people mark their quilts before the layers are assembled, some after. Marking

the quilt top before the three layers are basted together makes it easier to write on and allows you to easily trace over a pattern under your fabric if both layers are placed on a light box.

There are many possible tools for tracing patterns on the quilt top, including a dressmaker's pencil or chalk, and dressmaker's carbon paper. Avoid so-called erasable pens as they sometimes leave a line that eventually becomes yellow. I learned this the hard way!

BASTING THE QUILT LAYERS

Before you quilt, you need to baste the layers of your quilt together to keep them from moving around while you work. To baste the quilt layers together, tape the backing fabric on your work surface wrong-side up. Center the batting on top of the backing and center the quilt top, face up, on the batting. Using a hand sewing needle and a color of thread that is easily visible on your quilt top, baste the three layers together, starting from the center and working out in rays from the center, smoothing out any wrinkles as you go. If you prefer, you could pin-baste the quilt layers together instead, using small safety pins, about 4 inches apart, to secure the layers. There's a gadget called a basting spoon that helps you to push closed the many pins you will need for pin-basting, if you choose that method. Work from the center out for pin-basting as well.

Run a line of basting stitches about ¼ inch in from the edge of the quilt top after the center is basted. Trim any excess of the batting and backing that extends beyond the quilt top if you are using separate binding. If you are using the "Backing as Binding" method, don't trim the excess backing fabric and see page 18 to proceed.

MACHINE QUILTING

Quilting not only serves to hold the three layers of the quilt together and stabilize them, but also adds to the beauty of a quilt. There are hundreds of quilting patterns, both old and new, many derived from nature—for example, the outline of a pumpkin seed, a leaf, or a feather. (You can invent your own, also.)

As we're emphasizing speed here, we'll concentrate on machine quilting. Choose a simple pattern for your early attempts (illu. 14).

The first few times that you try machine quilting, it may not turn out the way you want it to, so practice on a couple of old bed sheets with batting in between. The key to success is learning to handle all the bulk. Try using longer stitches and a walking foot. (With a walking foot, the weight of your quilt will not create a drag on your machine, and you won't have to pull or push the quilt through the machine.) Using clear thread on your quilt top is a good idea when you have to quilt through different colors of fabric. You may have to loosen the top thread tension to get an even stitch.

A good job of machine quilting starts with good preparation. Lay your backing face down on a flat surface. Spread your batting out evenly over the backing and place your quilt top over it, face up. Make sure everything is smooth and pin-baste or thread-baste the layers together. Then, starting with the sides, roll or fold the left side of the quilt toward the center. (To hold the rolls in place, use quilt clips, bicycle clips, safety pins, or even plastic headbands.) Do the same with the right

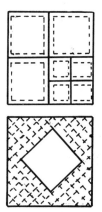

14. *Two simple quilting patterns. Top, outline quilting. Bottom, cross-hatching.*

side of your quilt, leaving a work area in the middle unrolled. Now fold your quilt accordion-style; this will allow it to sit nicely on your lap as you sew. As you finish quilting one part, unroll the part of the quilt to the right and continue quilting. When you have finished quilting the right half, reroll it, rotate the quilt 180°, and follow the same quilting procedure for the rest.

This is where a walking foot is helpful because you don't want the quilt to pull or create a drag. Turn your handwheel so as to draw the bobbin thread up to the top of the quilt. Start your stitch length at 0 and slowly move it to the desired length. Never backstitch—it looks sloppy. (Make sure to repeat this, only in reverse, when you're at the end of your quilting.)

You may want to quilt with a cross-hatch fill, a background design in which a series of parallel lines intersect to form Xes. Channel quilting is a lot like cross-hatch fill, except that it also includes quilt lines that run horizontally or vertically. Or do you want to use outline quilting? With outline quilting, you stitch ¼ of an inch away from both sides of the seamlines of your pieced work. Maybe you'd enjoy stitching in the ditch, using hidden stitching right on the seamline. For the above types of quilting, use a stitch length of 8 to 10 stitches per inch. How close together you place your quilting lines depends on several things, including the size of the quilt and the batting. For a small quilt, keep the quilt lines closer together. For a large quilt, they may look better further apart. Cotton batting needs to be quilted with lines no further apart than 3 or 4 inches; polyester batting may be quilted with lines 5 or 6 inches apart.

'Free-motion' quilting is a fun way to go. To do this, drop your feed dogs or cover them and use your hands to guide the fabric. Make sure that you don't reposition your quilt while sewing; this will cause puckering. I like to remove my pressure foot altogether, but I know there are those that like to use a darning foot when sewing free-motion. You don't need to worry about stitch length, because it is regulated by the speed and motion of your quilting. This technique works wonderfully when you use a template to add or create design, for soft curves or for filling in the background. The overall effect is beautiful even though there may be slight irregularities. Practice will reduce the amount of irregularities. We all seem to know babies that could use an everyday, beat-to-death quilt; we could give our practice one to one of them.

MACHINE TYING

Machine tying is an alternative to quilting. It secures the three quilt layers together only at the points where it is tied, giving the finished quilt a puffy look. It's a good idea to plan your tying points at regular intervals that complement the piecing of your quilt top. If you are using cotton batting, you need to tie every 2 or 3 inches. If you are using polyester batting, you can space the ties out further, every 5 to 6 inches.

First prepare the three layers as for basting: the quilt backing taped wrong-side up to your work surface, batting centered over the backing, quilt top face-up over the batting. Mark the tie points with a chalk pencil. Pin around the marks with small safety pins to pin-baste the quilt layers together, working outwards from the center of the quilt.

When you have finished marking and pinning the quilt, roll the sides of the quilt in towards the middle, with the quilt top facing up, so it resembles a scroll; secure with quilt clips. This will make it easier to maneuver the quilt in the machine. Set your sewing machine for a small zigzag stitch and lower the feed dogs. Lay a 4- to 6-inch piece of yarn or ribbon on the tie point. Then lower the presser foot and zigzag stitch over the yarn or ribbon, a procedure called *bar tacking*. Repeat this procedure at each tie point. When you are finished, clip the loose machine threads, remove all the pins, and slip knot each piece of yarn or ribbon.

HAND TYING

Like machine tying, hand tying is an alternative to quilting. I like to use embroidery floss to tie my quilts, but you can use yarn or even ribbon to join all three layers of your quilt.

You can decide to scatter your ties over the surface of your quilt, or you can use tailor's chalk and a ruler to mark out precisely where you want each tie. After deciding what to tie with and where to tie, you're ready to tie.

From the top side of your quilt, make a ¼-inch stitch through all three layers of the quilt with your floss or yarn, and come out on the top layer. Still working on the top, tie a double square knot. Cut and trim the ends of the floss so they are from ¾ inch to 1 inch long. (If I'm making a baby quilt, I always worry about the knots coming out and choking the baby. Before closing up each square knot, I add a drop of fabric glue. If you do this, always check the glue manufacturer's guidelines to be sure it's safe to eat, as this may happen.)

If you're using ribbon to tie your quilt, use a large needle that you can thread the ribbon through and very narrow ribbon. Working from the top of your quilt, make a ¼-inch stitch through all 3 layers. Make sure that you have equal amounts of ribbon of each side of the stitch. Form a slip knot with the ribbon, add a drop of fabric glue, and tie it in a bow. Trim off the ribbon ends to about 6 inches long, and go to the next tie point.

BINDING THE QUILT

I have three favorite ways of binding my quilts: bias binding, backing as binding, and the pillow method. The first two are done after the quilt has been quilted. The pillow method is done before quilting, which is usually done by tying the quilt.

Bias Binding

For the binding, choose a fabric that complements the quilt top. There are commercially available quilt bindings, or you could make your own.

Making Your Own Bias Binding. To make your own bias binding, you first need to make a square of the fabric. Lay the fabric you want to use for the binding on a flat surface, and find the 45° bias line (it is at 45° to the weave). Fold the fabric over as shown in illu. 15a into a triangle, making a sharp crease line. Trim off the excess beyond the folded square. Open out the fabric and cut the square in half on the crease line into two triangles (illu. 15b). Sew the two triangles together with right sides facing as shown in illu. 15c. Open out the fabric and iron it flat. Rule lines on the fabric that are the width across you want for your bias binding when unfolded (illu. 15d).

For single-thickness binding, the unfolded binding should be 4 times wider than

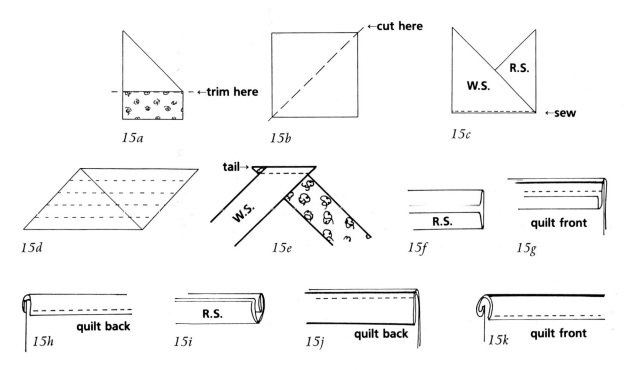

15. Bias binding. a: Squaring fabric for bias binding. b: Cutting the square in half. c: Sewing the triangles together. d: Ruling lines. e: Joining two sections of binding. f: Folding single-thickness binding. g: Stitching the first fold, single-thickness binding. h: Sewing the single-thickness binding to the quilt front. i: Folding double-thickness binding. j: Sewing double-thickness binding to the quilt back. k: Turn the binding over and stitch in place.

the finished binding is going to be. For example, if you want a 1-inch binding around your quilt, cut 4-inch-wide bias strips. With right sides together, stitch the sections of bias strip together to form one continuous strip as shown in illu. 15e. Cut off the "tails" at the seams after they are joined and iron the seam allowances open. Then fold your binding in half lengthwise, with right side out, and iron the fold flat. Unfold the binding.

Fold the outside long edges toward the center and press (15f). To sew the single-thickness binding to the quilt, open up the top fold of the binding and with the right side of the fabric towards your quilt back, machine stitch the binding to the quilt along the fold line (see illu. 15g). Turn the binding over the raw edges of your quilt and pin it in place on the front. Stitch it in place (illu. 15h). (Some people like to lay the binding on the front of the quilt top and machine stitch it in place, and then fold it toward the back and slipstitch it in place. This works wonderfully. I need to finish quickly, so I almost always use the first way.)

The second popular bias strip is the double-thickness bias strip. This is made by taking the width of the desired finished binding and multiplying it by six and cutting bias strips to that width, making sure that the fabric is cut on the true bias. Fold the strip in half lengthwise, with the right sides of the fabric outward. Then fold in thirds lengthwise and press (illu. 15i).

To sew the double-thickness binding to the quilt, open up the last two folds of the binding, and with the raw edges to the top, and the strip on your quilt back, machine stitch the binding to the quilt along the top fold (illu. 15j). Turn the binding over the raw edges of your quilt, pin in place on the front, and stitch it in place (15k). (As with the single-thickness binding, the double-thickness can also be machine stitched to the quilt front and then folded over to the back and slip-stitched in place.)

Backing as Binding

A second method of binding involves bringing the excess quilt backing, which extends beyond the quilt top, around to the front to serve as a binding. Choose a backing fabric that will complement your quilt top as a binding. The backing fabric should be 3 or 4 inches larger in each dimension than the quilt top. Before you bind the quilt, the three layers of backing, batting, and binding must be basted and quilted. For this method of binding, trim off any excess of the batting *only* (not the backing) that extends beyond the quilt top. Then trim the backing so that it extends 2 inches in each direction beyond the quilt top.

To bind the quilt, fold and press up a ¼-inch hem on the backing fabric; fold it towards the quilt top. Then turn over the excess backing to the front of the quilt and pin and stitch it in place by hand or by machine.

Pillowcase Method

This is a fast and easy way of finishing a quilt. It is done BEFORE the quilt is quilted, after you have pieced your quilt top. To assemble, lay your batting on your work surface. Then center your backing, face up, on it, and finally, center your quilt top face down over the backing. Baste all three layers together, ⅝-inch in from the edge of the quilt top. Trim off any excess batting and backing. Pin and sew through all three layers, ⅝-inch in from the edge of the quilt top, with your machine set for 10 to 12 stitches per inch; sew all the way around, except for a 3-foot turning opening on one side. After sewing, trim the batting close to the stitching to reduce bulk. Roll the corners and sides of the entire quilt unit tightly towards the opening you left, and pull the whole quilt through the opening between the quilt top and backing layers so it is turned right-side out. Flatten your quilt, and slipstitch the opening closed. Tying is a good method of finishing a quilt made by the pillowcase method (see pages 15 and 16).

HANGING YOUR QUILT

Once you have finished your quilt, you may want to hang it on the wall. You can use a pole or curtain rod, but it needs to be run through a cloth "sleeve" at the back of the quilt. (I put two sleeves on my quilts—one at the top and one at the bottom. See "Helpful Hints," page 20, to find out why.) To make a sleeve, cut a strip of cotton (it could be the same fabric as your quilt back) 8 inches deep and ·as wide as the quilt width minus 2 inches. Fold the strip in half lengthwise, wrong side out, and sew the long sides together with a ¼" seam allowance to make a tube. Hem the ends of the tube and turn it right-side out. Flatten the tube, center it on your quilt back near the top, and slipstitch it in place. Repeat this at the quilt bottom for the second tube.

Crazy Quilt (see page 85).

Other Useful Information

BED MEASUREMENTS

Before you begin your quilt, decide how large you want it to be. Do you wish it to cover only the mattress on your bed or to go beyond? Do you wish to pull it up over your pillows, or do you want to tuck it under the pillows? After you have decided what you want, measure your bed, both the length and the width. Bring your tape measure down from the bed top to where you want your quilt to end.

Here are some standard measurements for mattresses:*

Crib:	27 × 54 inches	Queen:	60 × 80 inches
Twin:	39 × 75 inches	King:	72 × 80 inches
Full:	54 × 75 inches		

These figures are the mattress sizes, not quilt sizes, but they should help you to decide how large to make your quilt and where you may need to add or subtract from a pattern to make your quilt fit.

HELPFUL HINTS

- Always prewash your fabrics
- Fabric fraying is usually a problem when you prewash. To prevent this, snip off a 45° angle on each corner. Make the cut only about 1 or 1½ inches deep.
- Trim off selvedges and discard them after washing the fabric.
- Set your machine for 10 to 12 stitches per inch for piecing
- When piecing, use quarter-inch seam allowances unless otherwise noted in patterns.
- For a lovely finished quilt, take the time to cut, sew, and press your pieces accurately.
- When joining two pieces that already have seams, press the seam allowances in opposite directions before joining the pieces to avoid bulk.
- When pressing seams, press them towards the darkest fabric to avoid a shadow behind the light colors.
- Do you need a ruffle for a pillow but hate to gather? Zigzag over a piece of twine or crocheting thread on the fabric you want ruffled; then pull the twine gently. It will gather neatly.
- Label quilts with your name and date. Here are some ways to do this: Use a permanent marker; cross-stitch the information on the quilt using waste canvas from counted cross-stitch; or take a piece of white cotton fabric and type the information on it; then slip-stitch the label in place on the quilt back.
- To keep the knots in place when tying your quilt, apply a drop of fabric glue over each one if you don't bar tack.
- When hanging a quilt on a wall, rotate it every six months or so. First hang it from the top, then from the bottom, since the constant pull on the threads can cause them to break.
- Share quilting with a friend.
- Make a heavy-duty template out of a plastic lid from a tub of soft margarine. If it is slippery, rough up the back a little with sandpaper.
- I hate rethreading my sewing machine every time I run out of thread, so I tie the end of the old thread to the start of the new thread. Then I continue to sew. As I'm sewing, the new thread will run through the machine, being pulled along by the old thread. When the knot arrives at the needle, I cut it off, thread my needle, and continue sewing.
- Never use nails or tacks to hang your quilts. Why put holes in your quilt? And eventually it will sag, making the holes even bigger.

*Sizes may vary from country to country.

- When storing your quilt, never keep it in plastic. Since plastic does not breathe, it allows moisture and insects to keep your quilt company until you air it out again.
- Air your quilt out and refold it in different directions every 3 or 4 months. Place it in a box lined with cotton sheets.

DESIGNING YOUR OWN QUILT

I try to always keep a small notebook with me; when I think of an idea or see something that I like or think would make a good quilt, I write it down. I never make detailed sketches unless it's important to the all-over idea. This can be done very quickly. Remember, you're not drawing a detailed blueprint; at this point your drawing can be loose. (In the case of the Wagon Tracks pattern, I'm glad I did carry a notebook, or that pattern and its beauty would have been lost to me and now to you.)

When you are ready, begin working up your sketches into a pattern. You need to decide if it will be appliquéd work or be made of pieced blocks. The standard size block for an appliquéd work is 10 inches. This way you're not overcome by too much area to fill. The standard size block for a pieced work is 12 inches. You're not tied into these measurements, as you can see by some of the block sizes for the patterns in this book. Take your sketch and a sheet of graph paper and transfer the sketch onto the graph paper. Make any adjustments so the design will fit into the desired block size. This is where the fun and excitement begins.

Decide if you want to speed piece your quilt top. If you do wish to speed piece, become well acquainted with the different speed techniques and have fun with them. Or do you have the time to piece traditionally?

When making a quilt, you want others to enjoy it as well as yourself. So allow everyone to enjoy the whole quilt first. Then they can focus in on details. To make this work, avoid making your quilt too busy, and avoid the thrown-together look. Some basic elements of design in quilting are texture, color, and size.

Texture: In most cases we can tell if something is smooth or rough just by looking at it. By placing different-textured fabrics next to each other, you can give the idea of depth. Or you can stimulate the viewer's eye in one area and allow it to move to less textured areas in the quilt.

Color: Color is used in design as a means to establish a mood for your quilt. Contrasting colors can be used to create a focal point.

Size of design: When you make a design large, don't fool yourself into thinking it will automatically be the focal point of the quilt. If you wish it to stand out, use color and/or texture contrasts to allow it to stand out.

GROUP QUILTING

Sometimes we may wish to make a group quilt for our parents or grandparents, and we want all the children to make blocks. Here are a few things to keep in mind:

- Stay organized; if there is to be a theme to the quilt, make sure all know what that theme is and that they are to stay within the limits of that theme. Decide on the size of the block and give each family or person two blocks of fabric of this size. In case of a mistake on one block, the person still has a spare; also all the background fabrics will match when reassembled.

- If anyone is in need of a design, children's coloring books are a wonderful source of ideas, with their nice clean lines and wide range of topics.
- Set a deadline for the return of the completed blocks so the blocks can be sewn together in time for the event. Try to give everyone between one and two months to complete his or her block. About one to two weeks before the deadline, telephone or drop each quilter a note as a reminder.
- Remember, quilting is a functional art form, so be creative.

*Basket Quilt
(Project 17).*

1. Fan Quilt

The fan quilt was popular between 1800 and the 1850s. The pattern that follows is a modern version of a traditional fan quilt. Approximate time to complete quilt top: 12 hours; fairly easy. Finished size 76 × 80 inches.

YARDAGE*

- 3 yards of Fabric A (black print)
- ²/₃ yard of Fabric B (light yellow)
- 1 yard *each* of Fabrics C, D, E, F, and G (blue, white print, pink, light green, purple)
- 3 yards of fusible interfacing (18 inches wide), or equivalent
- 5 yards of backing fabric
- 5 yards of batting (45 inches wide) or equivalent
- 1 yard of fabric to cut single-thickness bias strip or 1½ yards for double-thickness bias strip

*Colors in parentheses are colors in the model. Choose whatever colors are pleasing to you.

CUTTING

- Three 20 × 45-inch rectangles of Fabric A
- Three 20 × 22-inch rectangles of Fabric A
- Four 4 × 45-inch strips of Fabric B
- Nine 3 × 45-inch strips of *each* color: Fabrics C, D, E, F, and G
- Backing: Cut the backing in half to make two 2½-yard lengths and sew them together on a long side to make a 90 × 90 inch square
- Bias strip: See binding directions in "Speed Techniques" chapter.

DIRECTIONS

All piecing is done with ¼-inch seam allowances and right sides of fabric facing, unless otherwise noted.

1. To start, we will be working with 4 of each color of the 3 × 45-inch strips of fabrics C, D, E, F, and G (total 20 strips). Pair the strips off, mixing the fabrics, and sew each pair together on one long side. To be consistent, always sew with either the light or the dark fabric on top. Continue until all 20 strips have been sewn into pairs.

2. Trace out or photocopy the fan template; glue it to stiff cardboard, and cut it out. Stack your sewn C through G pairs of strips in piles of three pairs; they should still be wrong-side out and unpressed (illu. 1-1). Using the rotary cutter it will be easy to cut through all six layers. Line up the seams. Place the fan section template on top of all the strips; line up the seam on the template with the seams on the sewn strips, and cut out the fan section through all six layers (illu. 1-2). You need to make 44 2-fabric fan sections. (You will have extras. This is to ensure that you will have enough pieces. You can use the extras in a sampler quilt, a pillow, etc.) Press the sections open, with seam allowances towards the darker fabric.

3. Sew three of your 2-fabric fan pieces together on their long sides to form a fan (illu. 1-3). Repeat to make a total of 12 whole fans. This will use 36 2-fabric

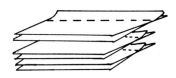

1-1. Three layers of strips, stacked for cutting fans.

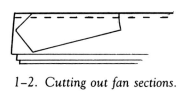

1-2. Cutting out fan sections.

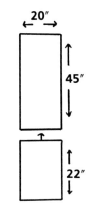

1-5. Joining panel pieces.

1-3. Piecing fans.　　　*1-4. Piecing corner units.*

fan sections. Pair off the remaining 8 fan sections and sew two sections together (illu. 1-4) to make a unit of four fabrics. Repeat with the other six 2-fabric fan sections. These are the corner pieces for the pieced border (see photo).

4. Read the section on speed appliqué in the "Speed Techniques" chapter. Using fusible interfacing, follow the directions given and back all whole 12 fans with interfacing. (You will have extra interfacing left over, in case you make a mistake.) Set them aside.

5. Take a 20 × 45-inch Fabric A rectangle and a 20 × 22-inch Fabric A rectangle. Sew them together on their 20-inch sides to make a panel (illu. 1-5). Repeat to make a total of three panels. Number them Panel 1, 2, and 3 (illu. 1-6).

6. Working with Panel 1, pin Fan H, face up, in place and cut the fan to align with the edge of the panel (illu. 1-6). Do the same with fans I and J. (Save the cut pieces of fan for Panel 2.) Press the fans in place on the panels to fuse the interfacing. Sew as directed in the "Speed Appliqué" section.

7. To make the joiner strips between the panels, sew two Fabric B strips together on a short side. Sew another two together the same way. Trim the joiner strip to the same length as the length of Panel 1.

8. Sew a joiner strip to the right-hand side of Panel 1, and set the unit aside. Follow illu. 1-6 again for Panel 2. Pin, press, and appliqué the fans and fan pieces in place. Sew the joiner that is attached to the right side of Panel 1 to the left side of Panel 2. Sew the second joiner strip to the right side of Panel 2. Set the unit aside.

9. Panel 3 is done in the same way as the other two. Press and appliqué the last fans and fan pieces in place. Sew the joiner that is attached to the right side of Panel 2 to the left side of Panel 3. This completes the quilt center.

10. To make the borders, we will work with the remaining twenty-five 3 × 45-inch strips of fabrics C through G. Sew five strips together lengthwise into a sheet, using one strip of each of the fabrics. Repeat this for a total of 5 sheets, joining the strips in the same order throughout. Square up the top ends of the sheets,

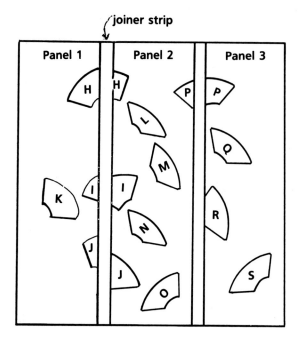

1-6. *Construction diagram, quilt center.*

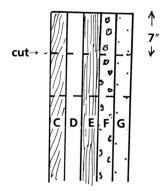

1-7. *Cutting border strip units.*

across the strips, if they aren't straight. Press.

11. Measure down 7 inches from the top of a pieced sheet (from Step 10) and cut across all 5 strips (see illu. 1-7). Continue cutting until all 5 sheets have been cut into 7-inch-long pieces. (There are enough of these border pieces to make a complete pieced border, just in case you don't want to add a fan in each corner, as was done in the model.)

12. Measure the side of your quilt center; set it aside. Sew the cut border pieces together on their 7-inch sides, joining them so that the colors fall into a repeating sequence. Connect enough border pieces to equal the length of the quilt side whose border you are making. Sew the pieced border to the side of the quilt center. Repeat this process for the opposite side of the quilt center.

13. For the top and bottom borders, measure across the top and bottom of the quilt just inside the edge of your newly attached side borders (about ½" down from the edge). This avoids any stretching at the edge that may give you a distorted measurement. Sew enough 7-inch pieced border units together to make a border that fits across the width of the top and bottom of your quilt center (but not out to the edges of the side borders if you plan to include the fan sections at the corners). Attach the top and bottom borders to the quilt top. This will leave a vacant square in each corner of your quilt top.

14. Working with one of the four fan corner pieces left over from when we were making our fans (Step 3), place it face down in one of the top corners. Line up the center pieced fan seam with the corner angle of the quilt top (illu. 1-8). Pin it in place to make sure nothing slides. Stitch around the center curve of the fan, starting ¼ inch from the long edge and ending within ¼ inch of the far long edge (illus. 1-8). Remove your pins and flip the fan over so it is right-side up. (See how it fills the vacant corner?) Turn the raw side edges of the fan under ¼ inch. Pin them in place on the border and stitch them in place (illu. 1-9). Repeat this process for the remaining three corners.

15. You are now ready to finish your quilt. For backing this quilt, I recommend the pillowcase method (see the chapter on "Speed Techniques"). Snip the corner seam allowances close to the seam to reduce bulk at each of the fan folds on the border before turning the sewn batting–backing–quilt top unit right-side out. Quilt by tying.

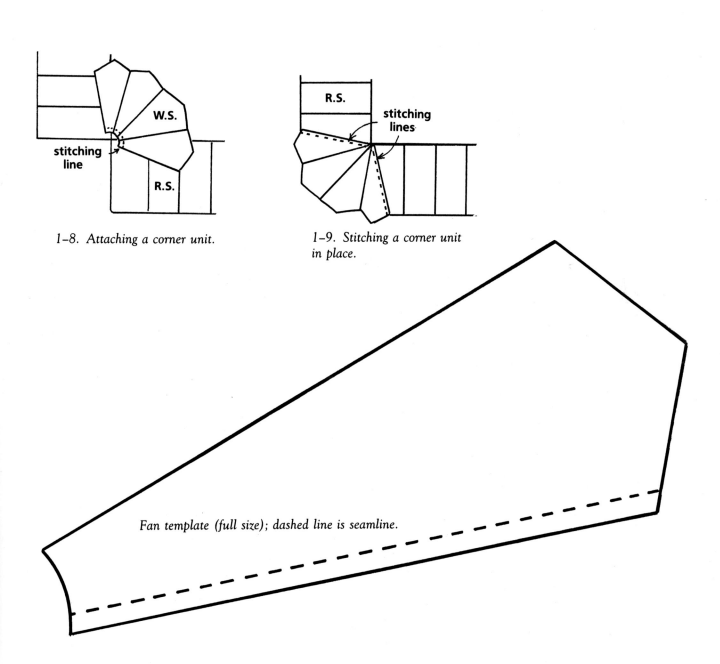

1-8. Attaching a corner unit.

1-9. Stitching a corner unit in place.

Fan template (full size); dashed line is seamline.

2. Roman Squares

Allover quilts, in which a simple unit is repeated all over the quilt top, are among the earliest quilts made in the United States, having been made since the 1750s. The love for European whole-cloth quilts had captured the hearts of many quilters in the early days, however, so it wasn't until the 1800s that the allover quilt finally came into its own. When they are made with a blend of different colors and textures, arranged in a pleasing geometric pattern, allover quilts can be very beautiful. Roman Squares is such a quilt. Approximate time to complete the quilt top: 8 to 10 hours; easy. Finished size: 78 × 96 inches.

YARDAGE*

- 3 yards of dark scraps (fabrics should be 45 inches wide)
- 1½ yards of light scraps (fabrics should be 45 inches wide)
- ⅔ yard of Fabric A (white)
- 1 yard for the inner border (purple floral)
- 1½ yards for the outer border (black floral)
- 5½ yards of backing fabric
- 5½ yards of batting (45 inches wide) or equivalent
- 1¼ yards of fabric to cut single-thickness bias strips or 1¾ yards for double-thickness bias strips

*Colors in parentheses are the colors in the model. Choose whatever colors are pleasing to you.

CUTTING

- Forty 2½ × 45-inch strips from the dark scraps
- Twenty 2½ × 45-inch strips from the light scraps
- Fifteen 7 × 7-inch squares of Fabric A; then cut 14 squares in half on the diagonal into large triangles; cut the remaining square into quarters on the diagonal for the small triangles.
- Eight 4 × 45-inch strips for the first (inner) border
- Nine 6 × 45-inch strips for the second (outer) border
- Backing fabric: Cut into two 2¼-yard pieces and seam them together lengthwise to be 90 inches across.
- Binding: See binding directions in "Speed Techniques" chapter

DIRECTIONS

Note: All construction is done with ¼-inch seam allowance and right sides of fabric facing, unless otherwise noted.

1. Take 20 dark and 20 light 2½ × 45-inch strips. Pair off a dark strip and a light strip, and sew them together lengthwise on one side. Repeat for a total of 20 times to make twenty 2-strip units.

2. Place your newly sewn 2-strip piece face up on the sewing machine bed with the light-colored strip closest to the needle. Take another dark 2½ × 45-inch strip and lay it face down over the light strip, aligned at right. Sew them together along their length at the right (with ¼-inch seam allowance) to make a 3-strip unit. Repeat for a total of twenty 3-strip units. Press them open, with seam allowances towards the dark fabrics.

3. Square up the short edge of a 3-strip unit. Measure across the top of your 3-strip unit. It should measure 6½ inches across. If it does, measure down 6½ inches and cut (illus. 2-1) across all 3 strips. (If it doesn't, measure down an equal distance to the strip's width and cut. You want to make a square.) Continue cutting the full length of your strip into squares. Repeat the cutting process for all twenty 3-strip units. You will have some extra, which can always be used in other projects (pillow shams, throw pillows, etc.).

4. Look at the construction diagram (2-2). Follow it as a guide for assembling

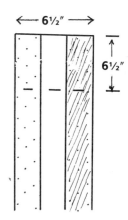

2-1. Cutting strip units.

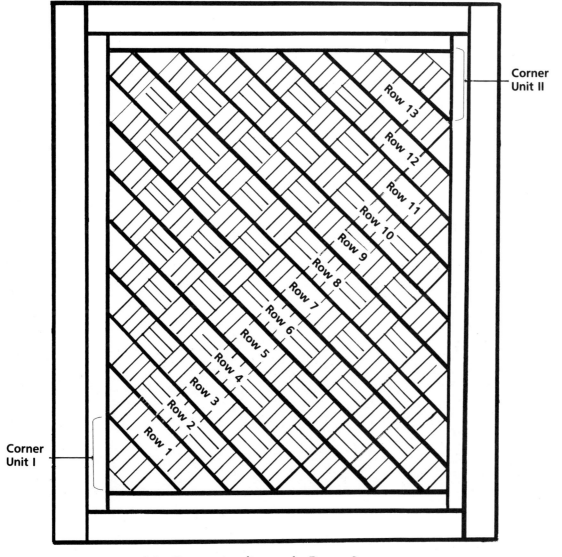

2-2. Construction diagram for Roman Squares.

Roman Squares.

your blocks and triangles (steps 4 through 9). The rows and corner units are set diagonally from lower right to upper left. Assemble and stitch together the rows as follows:

5. The corner unit (Unit I) has a small triangle (white in the model) on the top and a large triangle on each side of the pieced block (illu. 2-3).

6. Row 1 has 3 pieced blocks. The first and the third block should be laid in the same direction as the pieced block in the corner unit. Sew one large triangle on each end of Row 1.

7. Row 2 has 5 pieced blocks. *Note: Each odd-numbered block in the quilt top will be set with its stripes running in the same direction as the odd-numbered blocks in Row 1.* Seam one large triangle to each end of Row 2.

8. The piecing of the rest of the rows proceeds in the same way (see illu. 2-2):
Row 3: large triangle + 7 pieced blocks + large triangle
Row 4: large triangle + 9 pieced blocks + large triangle
Row 5: large triangle + 11 pieced blocks + large triangle
Row 6: large triangle + 13 pieced blocks + small triangle
Row 7: large triangle + 13 pieced blocks + large triangle
Row 8: small triangle + 13 pieced blocks + large triangle
Row 9: large triangle + 11 pieced blocks + large triangle
Row 10: large triangle + 9 pieced blocks + large triangle
Row 11: large triangle + 7 pieced blocks + large triangle
Row 12: large triangle + 5 pieced blocks + large triangle
Row 13: large triangle + 3 pieced blocks + large triangle

9. The last unit is Corner Unit II, which is just like Corner Unit I made in Step 5.

10. Read the section on adding borders in the "Speed Techniques" chapter for instructions on cutting and sewing borders. When you sew on the first border, remember that the triangles at the end of each row are cut on the bias, so be careful not to stretch them when sewing; bias-cut fabrics stretch easily. Attach the borders and finish the quilt as you like.

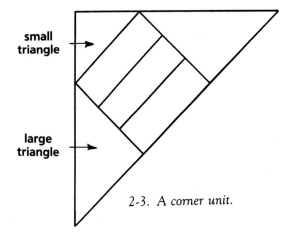

small
triangle

large
triangle

2-3. A corner unit.

3. Chimney-Sweep Quilt

When you look at this pattern, it's not too hard to see how it got its name. It's a lot like looking down a chimney, and who else but a chimney-sweep would be looking down a chimney.

Album quilts, also called "hospital quilts," were a standard way to raise money for charity. The patches or blocks were sold; then the buyer's signature was embroidered on the patch or block. The blocks were sewn together to form a quilt that was used in the hospital. (By tradition, the strips or patches were cut three inches wide.) Approximate time to complete the quilt top: 12 to 14 hours; easy. Finished size: 78″ × 78″. The quilt center is made up of 16 pieced blocks and 9 solid-colored blocks (white in the model). Finished block size: 11 × 11 inches without seam allowance. Finished quilt size: 75 × 75 inches.

YARDAGE*

- 2½ yards of Fabric A (white)
- 1½ yards of Fabric B (black-and-pink print)
- 1 yard for the first (inner) border (white with pattern)
- 1 yard for the second (middle) border (lavender)
- 1 yard for the third (outer) border (wine-colored)
- 4¾ yards of backing fabric (your choice)
- 4¾ yards of batting (45 inches wide) or equivalent
- Binding: 1 yard to cut single-thickness binding; 1½ yards to cut double-thickness binding

*Colors in parentheses are the colors in the model. Choose whatever colors you please.

CUTTING

- Fourteen 2½ × 45-inch strips of Fabric A
- Nine 12 × 12-inch squares of Fabric A
- One 6½ × 45-inch strip of Fabric A
- Two 2½ × 45-inch strips of Fabric B
- Two 6½ × 45-inch strips of Fabric B
- Six 4½ × 45-inch strips of Fabric B
- Eight 3½ × 45-inch strips for the first (inner) border*
- Eight 4 × 45-inch strips for the second (middle) border*
- Eight 4¼ × 45-inch strips for the third (outer) border*
- Backing: for a square quilt, cut the backing fabric into two 2⅜-yard (85.5-inch) lengths, and seam the lengths together to make a 90 × 85.5-inch backing.
- Binding: See binding directions in the "Speed Techniques" chapter

*If you want your quilt to be longer than it is wide, increase the width of the top and bottom borders. In that case, wait until you have assembled your quilt center to cut your borders.

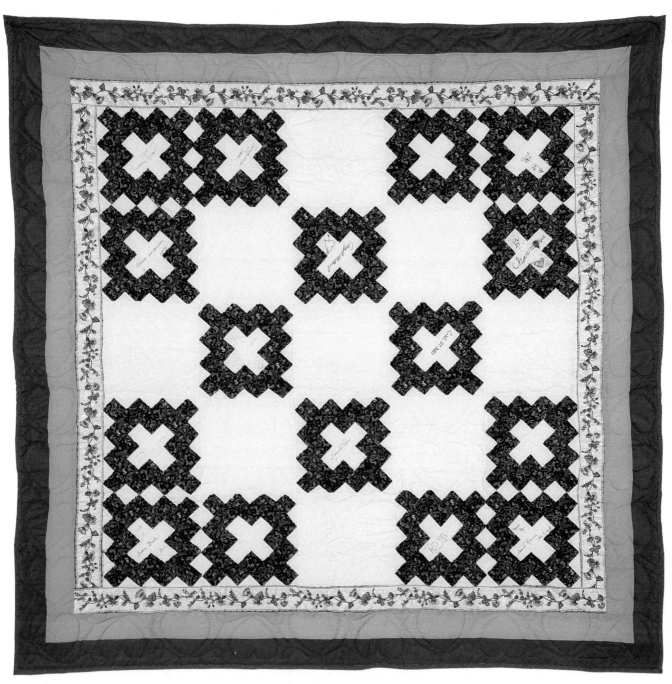

Chimney-Sweep Quilt

Signature quilts, or album quilts, were used as a way to keep records of family and friends. They begin to gain popularity around 1830, perhaps as a result of the westward movement that scattered many families in the U.S. The artist would have family and friends sign the quilt; this way the family would always be with her wherever she went.

DIRECTIONS

All construction is done with right sides of fabric facing and ¼-inch seam allowances, unless otherwise noted. Tag your block rows with masking tape as you make them, to avoid confusion later on when assembling. First we will piece the corners and rows that make up the pieced blocks. Illu. 3-1 shows how they will be assembled into blocks later.

1. Place a 2½-inch-wide Fabric A strip, face up, on your sewing machine bed. Top it with a 2½-inch-wide Fabric B strip, face down, and sew the lengths together on one long side. Open this sewn piece up and place it face up on your sewing machine bed with the Fabric B strip closest to the needle. Lay a 2½-inch-wide Fabric A strip face down over the B strip, aligned at right and sew them together at the right to make a 3-strip unit (illu. 3-2). Press it open, and measure down from the top 2½ inches; cut across all three strips (see illu. 3-2). Continue cutting the length of the pieced strips into 2½-inch units. Assemble three more A-B-A strips (each 2½ inches wide) and cut them in the same way. You'll need a total of 32 cut pieces, two for each of the 16 pieced blocks. These will become the corner units.

2. Look at illu. 3-3. This is going to be the corner of the block, which we'll make from the units pieced and cut in Step 1. Starting a quarter of an inch outside the seam line, cut your end (Fabric A) squares off at a 45° angle. (Save the triangles cut off.) Repeat this process for all of the 32 pieced units from Step 1.

3. For each unit trimmed in Step 2, take one of the triangles that was cut off and sew it on the top of the unit, above Fabric B (see illu. 3-4). Throw away the excess triangles. Press the units and set them aside.

4. Place a 2½-inch-wide Fabric A strip face up on your sewing machine. Top it with a 6½-inch-wide Fabric B strip, face down, aligned at right. Sew them together

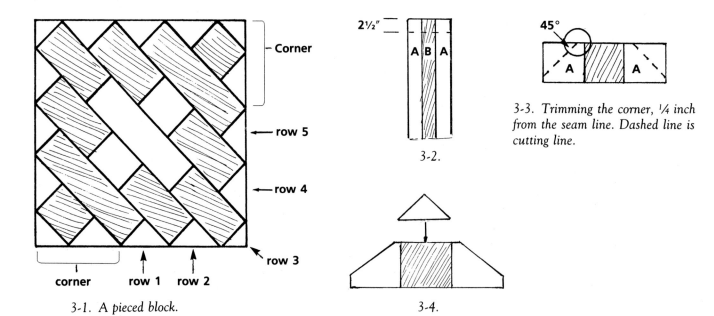

3-1. A pieced block.

2½"

A B A

3-2.

45°

3-3. Trimming the corner, ¼ inch from the seam line. Dashed line is cutting line.

3-4.

along one long side. Then open up this sewn unit and place it, face up, on your sewing machine with the Fabric B strip closest to the needle. Lay a 2½-inch-wide Fabric A strip face down over the B strip, aligned at right, and sew them together on the outer long side to make a 3-strip unit (A-B-A); see illu. 3-5. Press the unit open; square up the top of the strip if necessary. Measure down from the top 2½ inches, and cut across all 3 strips (see illu. 3-5). Continue cutting the pieced strips into 2½-inch units.

5. Make another A-B-A sheet like the one in Step 4 and cut it into 2½-inch long units the same way (illu. 3-5). You'll need a total of 32 cut pieces, which will become rows 1 and 5 in the blocks (16 of each).

6. Cut the end squares of the units made in steps 4 and 5 in the same way you did for the corner units (illu. 3-6). (Throw away all the cut-off triangles.) This completes the row 1 and row 5 units; press them and set them aside.

7. Sew two sheets of strips in the following order: a 2½-inch-wide strip of Fabric A, a 4½-inch-wide strip of Fabric B, a 2½-inch-wide strip of Fabric A, a 4½-inch-wide strip of Fabric B, and a 2½-inch-wide strip of Fabric A (see illu. 3-7). Square up the ends of the strips at the top; measure down 2½ inches, and cut across all 5 strips to form a 5-piece unit. Continue cutting units until the end of each sheet. You will need 32 5-piece units (2 for each block). These will become rows 2 and 4 of the blocks. Trim the end blocks at a 45° angle as before, ¼-inch away from the seam line (see illu. 3-8). Cut eight 3-inch squares of Fabric A. Then cut them into quarters on the diagonals. Press the pieced units and set them aside.

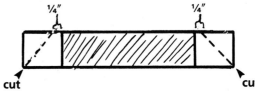

3-6. Trimming row 1 and 5 of the block, ¼ inch from the seam line. Dashed line is cutting line.

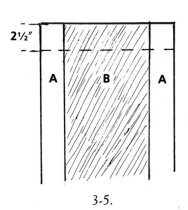

3-5.

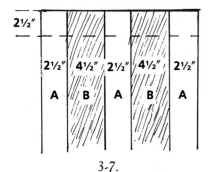

3-7.

3-8. Trimming row 2 and row 4 of the block, ¼ inch from the seam line. Dashed line is cutting line.

8. Next we'll make our last sheet of strips. We will need it to make Row 3 of the blocks. Sew one sheet of strips in the following order: a 4½-inch-wide strip of Fabric B, a 6½-inch-wide strip of Fabric A, and a 4½-inch-wide strip of Fabric B (see illu. 3-9). Press open the sheet and square off the top of the strips if necessary. Measure down 2½ inches, and cut across all 3 strips. Continue cutting 2½-inch units until you reach the end of the sheet. You will need one for each pieced block (16 units total). Cut triangles from the template and sew them to the ends of the Row 3 rows (see illu. 3-10).

9. Follow illu. 3-1 for block assembly as follows: Pin a corner unit to row 1, so they align to form a triangle, and sew the row to the corner unit.

10. Join the unit made in Step 9 to Row 2, and continue piecing the block, adding rows 3, 4, 5, and finally another corner unit. Assemble and sew the remaining 15 pieced blocks in the same way.

11. Assemble and sew the blocks to form the quilt top in rows (across), in the following order (the solid blocks are the squares of Fabric A):

Row One: 2 pieced blocks + 1 solid block + 2 pieced blocks

Row Two: pieced block + solid block + pieced block + solid block + pieced block

Row Three: solid block + pieced block + solid block + pieced block + solid block

Row Four: pieced block + solid block + pieced block + solid block + pieced block

Row Five: 2 pieced blocks + 1 solid block + 2 pieced blocks.

12. Read the section in the "Speed Techniques" chapter on adding borders. (If you want your quilt to be longer than it is wide, increase the width of the top and bottom borders.) Attach the borders and finish the quilt as you like.

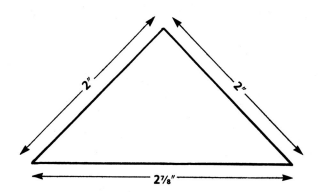

Template for corners of block row 3. Add ¼″ seam allowances.

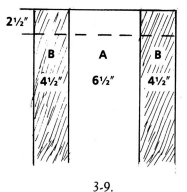

3-9.

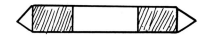

3-10. Row 3, with triangles at the ends.

4. Schoolhouse

The schoolhouse was very dear to the pioneer mother. She knew, as a mother knows today, that education would always be with her child. When she reached her destination after the long journey west, one of the first things that she insisted on was a schoolhouse for her children. For many years in each new community, the only schoolhouse was filled with children ranging from ages 6 to 16, sitting side by side in one room and studying.

Traditionally, the Schoolhouse pattern was worked in Turkey red (a red dyestuff originally made from the roots of the madder plant). Nowadays, the imagination of our creative quilters has allowed many types of houses, and other buildings, for that matter, to grace their quilts. The traditional Schoolhouse pattern that follows dates to around 1830 to 1840; the quilt top is made of 24 pieced blocks, in 6 rows with 4 blocks in each row, separated by sashing. It has one border. Approximate time to complete the quilt top: 2 to 3 days; a challenge, but worth it. Quilt size: 65 × 94 inches. Finished block size, about 10½ (width) × 11 inches (length).

YARDAGE*

- 3¾ yards of Fabric A (red)
- 3¾ yards of Fabric B (white)
- 5½ yards of backing
- 5½ yards of batting (45 inches wide) or equivalent
- 1 yard of fabric to cut single-thickness bias binding or 1¾ yards of fabric to cut double-thickness bias binding

*Colors in parentheses are the colors in the model. Choose whatever colors please you.

Note: A cutting mat with a 1″ grid is recommended for this project. Safety-pin same-width strips together and label to avoid confusion after cutting.

CUTTING

- Two 3¾ × 45-inch strips of Fabric A
- Sixteen 1½ × 45-inch strips of Fabric B
- Thirty 1½ × 45-inch strips of Fabric A
- Three 4½ × 45-inch strips of Fabric A
- Two 4½ × 45-inch strips of Fabric B
- Eight 2½ × 45-inch strips of Fabric B
- Two 2¼ × 45-inch strips of Fabric B
- Four 2 × 45-inch strips of Fabric A
- Two 3 × 45-inch strips of Fabric A
- Two 2¾ × 45-inch strips of fabric A
- Four 2 × 45-inch strips of Fabric B
- Twenty-two 3 × 45-inch strips of Fabric B
- Eight 6¼ × 45-inch strips of Fabric A for border

DIRECTIONS

All piecing is done with right sides of fabric facing and ¼-inch seam allowances, unless otherwise noted. The triangle template given includes ¼-inch seam allowances.

1. Each part of the quilt block is labelled in illu. 4-1 for ease of understanding. First we will cut the C triangles. Trace out the triangle template provided, back it on strong cardboard, and cut it out of the cardboard. Take the two 3¾ × 45-inch Fabric A strips and trace and cut out 24 C triangles from them. Make sure to mark on each triangle where the base of the triangle is. See illu. 4-2 for one speed cutting method.

2. Next we'll be making the roof peak units (C + D); see illu. 4-3. Place a 1½ × 45-inch Fabric B strip face up on your sewing machine bed with one short end at the top. One inch from the top edge of the strip, lay a C triangle face down. Pin it in place so its edge is aligned with the right side of the strip and the triangle's base is at the top left (see illu. 4-4 for placement). Pin other triangles below it on the strip in the same way, leaving 1 inch of strip empty beyond the last triangle attached to each strip. About nine will fit on a strip. Stitch the triangles to the strip at the right edge with ¼-inch seam allowance. Repeat to join a total of 24

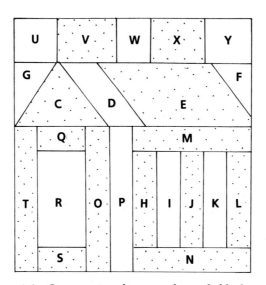

4-1. Construction diagram of a quilt block.

Key

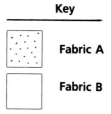

Fabric A

Fabric B

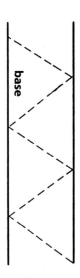

4-2. Speed cutting of triangles. Dashed lines are cutting lines.

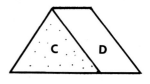

4-3. A roof peak unit.

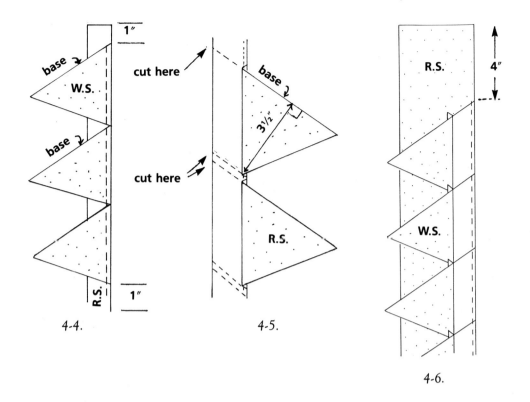

4-4.

4-5.

4-6.

triangles. Press the unit open with the seam allowances towards the triangle. Draw a cutting line that extends the base of each triangle onto the strip, as shown in illu. 4-5. Draw another line from the triangle's point onto the strip, parallel to the extended base line. Measured from the base line (at a right angle to the base line), the top line, from the triangle's point, is 3½ inches away (see illu. 4-5). Pressing and using the one-inch grid lines on your cutting mat as a guide is a must to keep everything straight. Use these guides throughout the pattern; if you don't, it won't come out as nicely as you would like it to. Cut along the lines you just drew to make the C+D units.

3. Set a 4½ × 45-inch Fabric A strip face up, with the short end up, on your machine bed. Lay one CD unit face down over it, 4 inches down from the top edge of the strip, and stitch it in place ¼" in from the right edge (see illu. 4-6). Keep butting in new C+D pieces in the same way, until the strip is filled (about 9 units). Repeat until all 24 CD units have been attached to 4½-inch-wide Fabric A strips. Press the units open. With the fabric right-side up, extend the lines from the top and bottom of the roof peak unit onto the Fabric A strip (see illu. 4-7). The lines should be parallel to each other and 3½ inches apart if you measure at a right angle to the extension of the base line of the triangle (see illu. 4-7). The pieces marked on the strip will become the E pieces in the block. Mark and cut 24 of these CDE units.

4. Put a 2½ × 45-inch Fabric B strip face up, with a short side on top, on your machine bed. Top it with a CDE unit face down (see illu. 4-8). The E piece should be pinned 2 inches down from the top of the strip (see 4-8), with the strip and pieced unit aligning at right. Stitch the E piece to the strip at the right with a ¼" seam allowance, as shown in illu. 4-8. Add in new CDE units as you sew

Schoolhouse

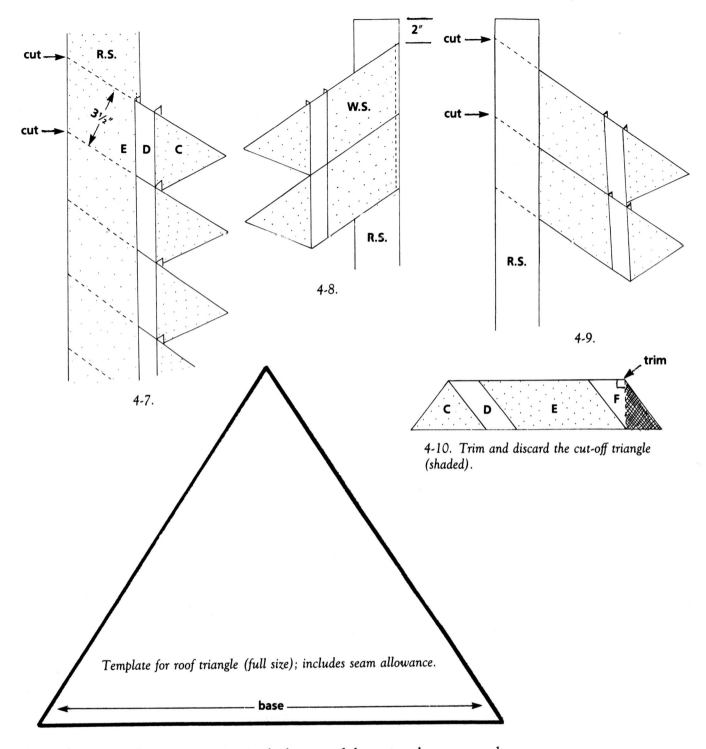

cut →   R.S.

3½"

cut →   E D C

4-7.

2"

cut →

W.S.

cut →

R.S.

4-8.

R.S.

4-9.

trim

C   D   E   F

4-10. Trim and discard the cut-off triangle (shaded).

Template for roof triangle (full size); includes seam allowance.

← base →

down the strip. Take new strips to attach the rest of the units when you need to, until all 24 CDE units have been attached to 2½-inch-wide Fabric B strips. Press the joined pieces flat and extend the lines at the top and bottom of the attached unit onto the 2½-inch strip, as shown in illu. 4-9. The lines should be 3½ inches apart. Cut along the lines. The strip just attached will make the F units in the block. Trim the CDEF units as shown in illu. 4-10.

5. Take another 2½ × 45-inch Fabric B strip, and lay it face up on your machine bed with a short end at the top. Place a CDEF unit face down over it, aligned at right as shown in illu. 4-11, with the C unit at the right. Stitch the CDEF unit in place at the right with ¼-inch seam allowances as shown (illu. 4-11). Add in the next CDEF units below it. Leave an extra 1 inch of strip uncovered beyond the last unit on the strip, however. Keep joining CDEF units to 2½-inch-wide Fabric B strips until you have joined 24 in all. Press the entire unit open and, on the right side of the fabric, extend lines from the base and top of triangle C onto the strip. The lines should be parallel and 3½ inches apart, when measured at right angles to the base line. Cut the strip on the lines you just drew. The pieces just added will become the G triangles. Mark the pieces just added as shown in illu. 4-12c, cut along the marked lines, and discard the pieces cut off. Press the unit flat and measure it. It should measure about 11 × 3½ inches (see illu. 4-12b). Set these units aside. You have just finished the hardest part of the pattern—the roof.

6. Next we'll make the windows. We'll be sewing three 1½ × 45-inch Fabric A strips to two 1½ × 45-inch Fabric B strips along their long sides, alternating them, as shown in illu. 4-13, to make a striped sheet of fabric. Make two more for a total of three sheets. Measure down 4½ inches from the top of a sheet and cut across all four strips (see illu. 4-13). You'll need to cut 24 of these 4-strip pieces. These will become the Schoolhouse windows (HIJKL). At this point, take a few minutes to make sure that everything fits together correctly. Lay (but don't sew) your windows under the roof of the house (GCDEF), and if the windows unit fits evenly at the far right edge and also extends to the left of the white roof strip about ½ inch, you're doing fine (see illu. 4-14). If the strips don't extend over, your seam allowances on the seams on the strips you just pieced may be too large. Adjust them as necessary.

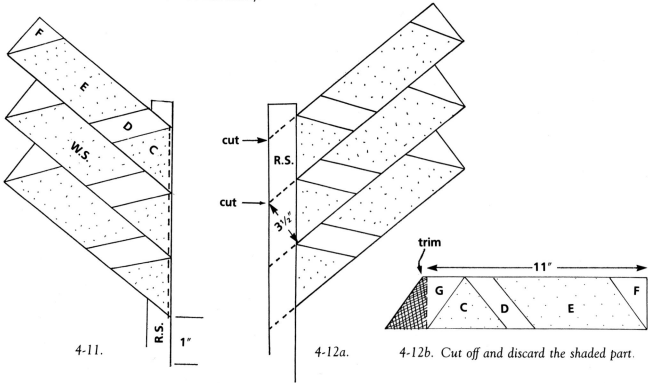

4-11.

4-12a.

4-12b. *Cut off and discard the shaded part.*

7. Now it's time to frame our windows. Place a 1½-inch-wide Fabric A strip face up on your sewing machine bed with a short end at the top. Lay one windows unit (HIJKL) on it face down, with its stripes going left to right (see illu. 4-15). Stitch the windows unit to the strip at their right edges, with ¼ inch seam allowances. Butt in new window pieces, using more strips as needed, until all 24 have been added to 1½-inch-wide Fabric A strips. Cut apart between the units (see illu. 4-15). You have just added an M piece. After cutting the units apart, we need to add a frame to the opposite side of each window (the N piece). Put another 1½-inch-wide Fabric A strip face up onto the sewing machine bed with its short end at the top, and put the unit you just pieced, wrong-side up, on top of it, with the stripes going right to left. Sew the units together at the right edge, with ¼-inch seam allowances, and cut the units apart as you did for the M pieces (see illu. 4-16). You have just framed in the top and bottom of your window (pieces M and N). Continue the framing for a total of 24 windows. Press the units open and set them aside for later use in Step 8.

8. Next, we'll be stitching the left side of the window frame (OP) to each window made in Step 7. Pair off a 1½-inch-wide Fabric A strip and a 1½-inch-wide Fabric B strip. Sew them together lengthwise with right sides of fabric facing,

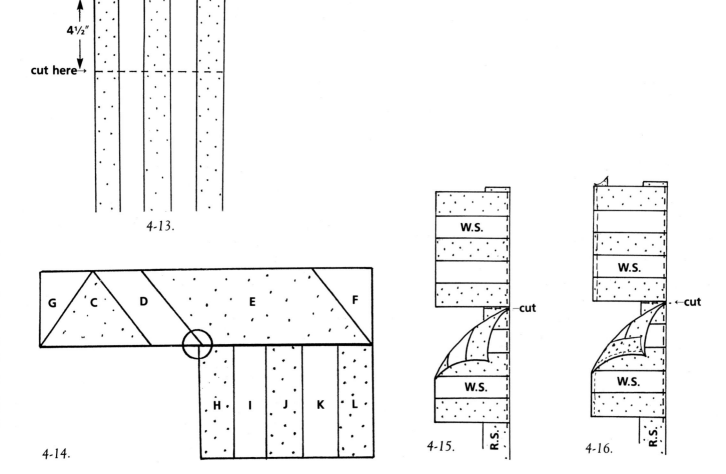

4-13.

4-14.

4-15.

4-16.

on one long side. Repeat for a total of four 2-strip units. Press them open. Lay the two-strip unit face up on your sewing machine bed with the Fabric B strip at the right (illu. 4-17). Place a window unit from Step 7 face down with the stripes running the same way. Add the new window units below the first one on the strip, taking new strips when needed, until the window units have all been added to your two-strip units. Cut the units apart across the two-strip unit, as seen in illu. 4-17, and press open. They should look like the unit in illu. 4-18. Set the units aside.

9. With the right sides of fabric together, pair off a 4½-inch-wide Fabric B strip and a 1½-inch-wide Fabric A strip. Sew them together on one long side. Make another two-strip unit the same way. Take another 1½-inch-wide Fabric A strip and sew it next to the Fabric B strip of each two-strip unit just made, with right sides of fabric facing (see illu. 4-19). Press open. Measure down 2½ inches from the top of the strips and cut across all 3 strips as shown in illu. 4-19. Cut a total of twenty-four 3-strip units the same way. They will be QRS in the block. Press them open. Sew the QRS pieces to the O strip side of the units shown in illu. 4-18, with right sides of fabric facing and ¼-inch seam allowances. When they are pressed open, the unit will look like illu. 4-20. Make 24 of these units. You've just added the doors to your schoolhouses.

10. Let's finish up the bottom of our house by framing in the other side of the door (piece T in the block). Lay a 1½-inch-wide Fabric A strip face up on your machine bed with the short end at the top. Place the unit you made in Step 9 face

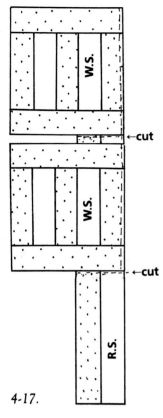

4-17.

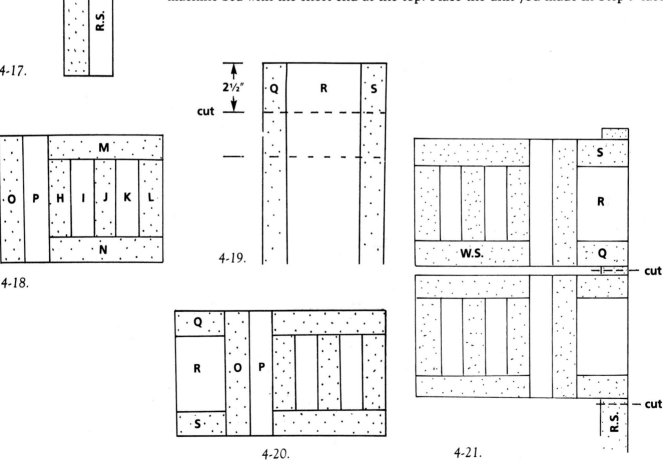

4-18.

4-19.

4-20.

4-21.

down over it with the "door" (QRS) to the right (illu. 4-21), and stitch the unit to the strip at the right side. Add in more units from Step 9 and sew them to the strip, until all the units from Step 9 have been joined to a 1½-inch-wide Fabric A strip. Cut the units apart across the strip so the finished house block unit will look like illu. 4-22. Take the roof units completed in Step 6 (see illu. 4-12b) and sew one to each house block with right sides of fabric facing (illu. 4-23). Press the units open and set them aside.

11. Next, let's sew our chimney row. First, sew the following strips together lengthwise to form a sheet of strips, with the usual ¼-inch seam allowances and right sides facing: a 2¼-inch-wide Fabric B strip, a 3-inch-wide Fabric A strip, a 2-inch-wide Fabric B strip, a 2¾-inch-wide Fabric A strip, and a 2½-inch-wide Fabric B strip (see illu. 4-24). Make another sheet the same way. Press them flat and measure down 2½ inches from the top of one. Cut all the way across the strips (see 4-24). This will make the UVWXY unit (see illu. 4-1). Cut 24 such units. Sew the UVWXY unit to the top of your schoolhouse (see illu. 4-25). Repeat to

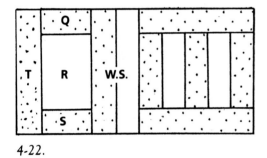

4-22.

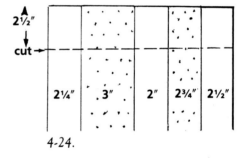

4-24.

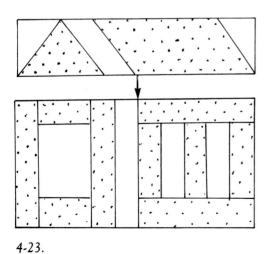

4-23.

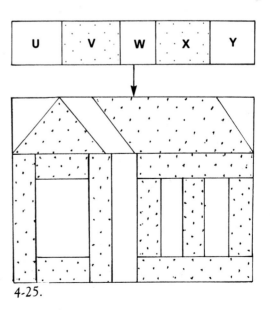

4-25.

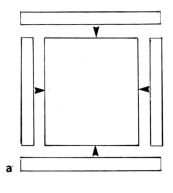

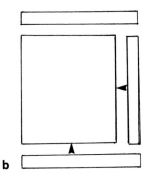

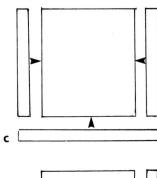

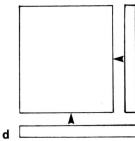

complete all 24 blocks. Even off the edges of your blocks. When done, they should measure about 11 (width) × 11½ inches (length) each; these measurements include the seam allowances. Now let's frame our blocks and finish our quilt.

12. To save on fabric, we cut the framing strips (3 × 45-inch strips of Fabric B) across the width of the fabric. Now sew all of them together at their short ends. This way there are no wasted ends cut off; they are used to finish framing the squares. Depending on where the block will go in the quilt, we will have four kinds of framing needs. See illu. 4-26 for the layouts of the frames and proceed as follows:

- Completely frame one block (see illu. 4-26a). This will go in the upper left-hand corner of our quilt center.
- On three of the blocks, frame the top, bottom, and right side of the blocks (illu. 4-26b). These will complete the top row of the quilt center.
- On 5 of the blocks, add a frame to both sides and the bottom (illus. 4-26c). These will be the starting blocks for rows 2 through 6.
- On 15 blocks, add a frame to the right side and the bottom (illu. 4-26d). These will fill in the rest of the quilt center.

See illu. 4-27 for the positions of the blocks, and sew them together in rows after they are framed, working from left to right across each row. Then join the rows together by sewing Row 1 to Row 2, etc.

13. Add a 6-inch Fabric A border all the way around the quilt top (see the "Speed Techniques" chapter section on adding borders). Finish the quilt as you like; refer to the "Speed Techniques" chapter for more information.

Row 1 ☐ ☐ ☐ ☐	**Key**
Row 2	☐ Completely framed: 1 block
Row 3	Top, bottom and right side framed: 3 blocks
Row 4	Both sides and bottom framed: 5 blocks
Row 5	Right side and bottom framed: 15 blocks.
Row 6	

4–27. Framing diagram for assembling rows of blocks.

4-26. a: Framing a block on 4 sides. b: Framing the top, bottom, and right side. c: Framed on both sides and bottom. d: Framed on right side and bottom.

46

5. Ohio Star

No native-grown cotton pieced works were found before the 1750s in the British colonies in North America; pieced works were all made of linen, silk, velvet, wool, and imported calico from India. During the 1750s, imported cottons from France and India, along with American-grown cotton, started to gain acceptance. Cotton later became a staple American crop. The wealthier landowners had spinning houses, where they would card wool and prepare it for spinning it into yarn or thread. But around 1769, when the Americans felt that they were unfairly taxed under the laws made and enforced by the British Parliament, spinning houses soon were transformed into weaving houses, where cotton was wound and woven for all the fabrics needed. Cotton quilts began to be commonplace. It was around this time that star patterns became popular. Stars have always been enjoyed by quilters. They gain acceptance, then fade from popularity, but they never really leave the scene altogether.

The Ohio Star given here is made of 5 rows of 4 blocks each, set without sashing (see illu. 5-1). I hope you enjoy it. Approximate time to complete the quilt top, 12 to 14 hours; fairly easy. Finished block size: 15 × 15 inches (without seam allowances). Quilt size: 71 × 86 inches.

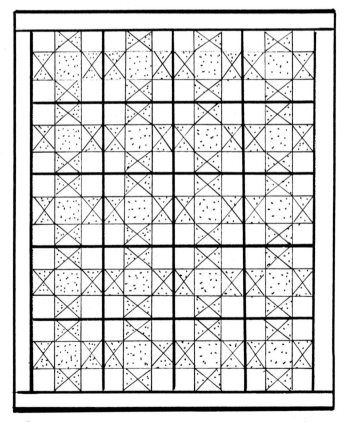

5-1. Construction diagram of quilt top. Thick lines show block divisions.

Ohio Star

YARDAGE*

- 3½ yards of Fabric A (white)
- 3½ yards of Fabric B (blue)
- 5 yards of backing fabric
- 5 yards of batting (45 inches wide) or equivalent
- 1 yard of fabric to cut single-thickness bias binding or 1¾ yards of fabric to cut double-thickness bias binding (if you are not quilting by the "pillow method")

*Colors in parentheses are the colors in the model. Choose whatever colors are pleasing to you.

CUTTING

- One 45 × 40-inch piece of Fabric A
- One 45 × 40-inch piece of Fabric B
- Three 5½ × 45-inch strips of Fabric B
- Twelve 5½ × 45-inch strips of Fabric A
- Eight 6 × 45-inch strips of Fabric B (for the border)
- Backing fabric: Cut into two 2½-yard lengths, and seam them in one long side to make a 90 × 90-inch backing
- Binding: See binding directions in the "Speed Techniques" chapter.

DIRECTIONS

All construction is done with right sides of fabric facing and ¼-inch seam allowances, unless otherwise noted.

1. In the "Speed Techniques" chapter, read the section on 4-triangle squares. Take the most easily marked 45 × 40-inch piece of fabric. Mark the wrong side of the fabric with a grid of 6⅜-inch squares (see illu. 5-2); make it 7 squares across

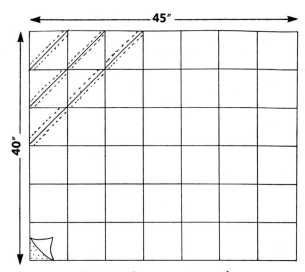

5-2. Marking a cutting grid.

5-3. A 4-triangle square.

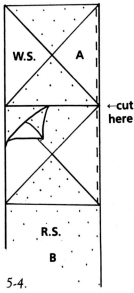

W.S.   A

←cut here

R.S.

B

5-4.

and 6 squares down. Pin the fabric to the second 45 × 40-inch piece of fabric with right sides facing. Mark, cut, and sew the squares into 4-triangle squares, as explained in the "Speed Techniques" chapter. You will need eighty 4-triangle squares for the quilt top (see illu. 5-3). Press the squares flat.

2. Place a 5½ × 45-inch Fabric B strip face up on your sewing machine bed with the short end at the top. Lay a 4-triangle square face down over it, making sure that one of the Fabric A triangles is to the right (see illu. 5-4). Sew the pieced square to the strip at the right with ¼-inch seam allowances. Continue adding pieced squares to 5½-inch-wide Fabric B strips until 20 4-triangle squares have been attached. Take new strips as needed. Cut across the strip between the pieced blocks (see illu. 5-4) to separate the units. The block pattern (illu. 5-5) shows where the C square (just added) is located in the block.

3. Sew a 4-triangle square to the empty side of the C square of each unit made in Step 2, a total of 20 times. The three joined squares should look like illu. 5-6. Press the units and set them aside. Each will become the central row of a block.

4. Put a 5½ × 45-inch Fabric A strip face up on your sewing machine bed with a short end at the top. Lay a 4-triangle square face down over it, being sure a Fabric B triangle is to the right (see illu. 5-7a). Continue sewing 4-triangle squares to the

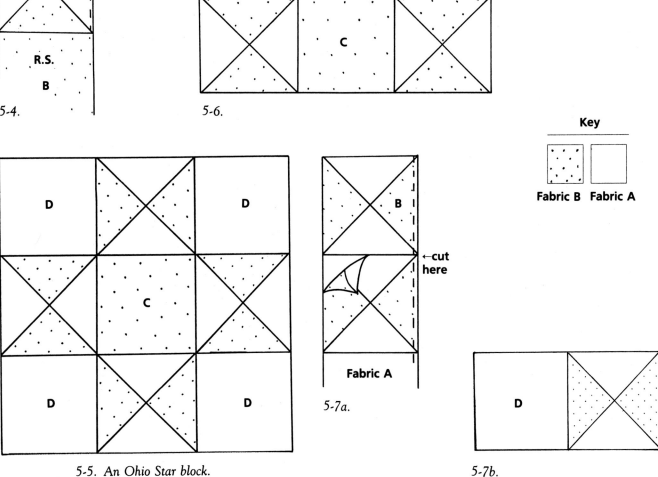

C

5-6.

D   D

C

D   D

5-5. An Ohio Star block.

B

←cut here

Fabric A

5-7a.

Key

Fabric B   Fabric A

D

5-7b.

strip, taking more 5½-inch-wide Fabric A strips as needed, until forty 4-triangle squares have been attached to strips. Cut across the strips between the squares (see illu. 5-7a). You have made units of D squares + pieced squares (see illu. 5-7b).

5. Place a 5½ × 45 inch Fabric A strip face up with the short side at the top on your sewing machine bed, and lay your newly sewn D square + pieced square unit face down over it, with the 4-triangle square aligned with the strip at the right (see illu. 5-8). Stitch them together at the right with ¼-inch seam allowances (illu. 5-8). Continue to sew in new D + pieced square units along the strip, taking more Fabric A strips when needed, until all 40 units have been sewn to 5½-inch-wide Fabric A strips. Cut the units apart across the strip; when finished the units will look like illu. 5-9. They will become the top and bottom rows of the blocks.

6. Take one central row, made in Step 3, and two rows made in Step 5. Join them as shown in illu. 5-10 to make a block. Repeat to make all 20 blocks.

7. Sew your completed blocks into five rows by joining one next to the other; each row has 4 blocks in it (illu. 5-1).

8. Sew your rows together to form the central part of the quilt top. Attach the borders and finish the quilt as you like. (See the "Speed Techniques" chapter for border and quilting instructions. (The model was completed by the "pillowcase" method.)

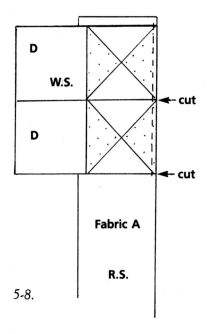

5-8.

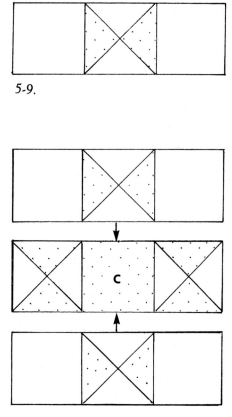

5-9.

5-10.

6. Log Cabin Variation

There is a traditional symbolism applied to the colors of the Log Cabin pattern. The red center square stands for the fireplace or the center of the home. The light side and the dark that many log cabin squares have stand for the lighter and darker sides of life. However, I have heard that the lighter and darker sides stand for the light and shadows thrown by the fire. If you should use a yellow center square, it is supposed to be a guest quilt, yellow representing the light in the window, put there for the weary traveller.

The Log Cabin pattern is one of the few that is not to be hand-quilted. This pattern is almost always tied. It is just too busy for elaborate hand quilting to show up. There are many variations of the Log Cabin, including the Pineapple, Patience Corner, and Courthouse Steps. The following pattern is a variation of the traditional Log Cabin quilt. It has Courthouse Steps blocks for the outer (white and red) blocks, as well as the traditional Log Cabin blocks in the pieced triangles around the large central red square (see construction diagram, illu. 6-1). Approximate time needed to complete the quilt top: 12 to 14 hours; fairly easy. Finished size, 76 × 76 inches. Size of a finished outer (red and white) Log Cabin block, 10½ × 10½ inches (without seam allowances).

6-1. Construction diagram, Log Cabin Variation.

YARDAGE*

- One 16½ × 16½ inch illustrated center panel (geese, in model)
- 2½ yards of Fabric A for borders and large triangles, and blocks (red)
- ¼ yard of Fabric B (white with pink print)
- ¼ yard of Fabric C (green)
- ½ yard Fabric D (white with blue print)
- ¼ yard Fabric E (dark blue print) for border around (red) triangles
- 2½ yards of Fabric F for outer blocks (off white, muslin)
- 1 yard of Fabric G for border and Sawtooth Bars (dark blue)
- 4¾ yards of backing
- 4¾ yards of batting (45 inches wide) or equivalent
- 1 yard of fabric for cutting single-thickness bias binding or 1½ yards for cutting double-thickness bias binding

*Colors in parentheses are colors in the model. Use whatever colors are pleasing to you.

CUTTING

- Four 8½ inch squares from Fabric A; then cut them in half on the diagonal to form 8 triangles
- Seven 2 × 45 inch strips of Fabric A
- Five 3 × 45 inch strips of Fabric A (for second inside border)
- Eight 4 × 45 inch strips of Fabric A (for second outside border)
- Two 2½ × 45 inch strips of Fabric B
- Three 2½ × 45 inch strips of Fabric C
- Four 2½ × 45 inch strips of Fabric D
- Four 1¾ × 45 inch strips of Fabric E
- 10 × 45 inch rectangle of Fabric F
- Fifteen 2 × 45 inch strips of Fabric F
- Two 3½ × 45 inch strips of Fabric F
- Two 6½ × 45 inch strips of Fabric F
- Two 9½ × 45 inch strips of Fabric F
- 10 × 45 inch rectangle of Fabric G
- Eight 3 × 45 inch strips of Fabric G, for first outer border (dark blue in model)
  - Backing: Cut into two lengths of 2⅜ yards and seam together along side to make a 90 × 85.5 inch backing
- Binding: See binding directions in the "Speed Techniques" chapter.

DIRECTIONS

All piecing is done with right sides of fabric facing and ¼-inch seam allowances, unless otherwise noted.

1. Working with your 8 Fabric A triangles, pair them off and sew each pair together on a short side (illu. 6-2). Press them open and sew one pieced triangle to each side of your center illustrated panel so that it will look like the center of illu. 6-3. Then read the section on adding borders in the "Speed Techniques" chapter, and add Fabric E strips as a border to all four sides of the square you just made (see 6-3). Remember that the triangles were cut on the bias, so be careful not to let the fabric stretch. Set the unit aside.

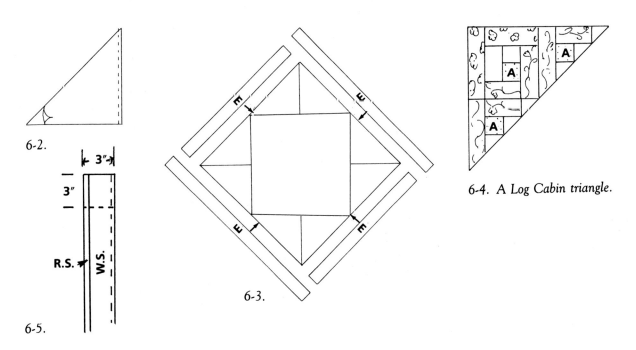

6-2.

6-3.

6-5.

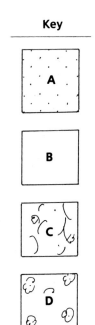

6-4. A Log Cabin triangle.

Key

A

B

C

D

Making the Log Cabin Triangles (illu. 6-4)

First we will build the blocks for the triangles, starting from the A square and working out in a speed-piecing method called *railroading*.

2. Place a 3-inch-wide Fabric A strip face up on your sewing machine, with a short end toward you. Cover it with a 2½-inch-wide Fabric B strip, face down, aligning them at the right, and sew them together at the right (illu. 6-5). Then measure down 3 inches from the top and cut across both strips; repeat to cut a total of eight AB pieces. Press the unit.

3. Lay a 2½-inch-wide Fabric B strip face up on your sewing machine bed, with a short end toward you. Place one of your newly sewn AB pieces face down over it, aligned at the right, making sure that the Fabric B piece is to the top (illu. 6-6a). Sew it to the strip at the right; butt in new AB pieces until all eight have been added to the Fabric B strip. Cut them apart across the strip as shown in illu. 6-6a. Press the units (the BBA blocks) open. They will look like 6-6b.

4. Set a 2½-inch-wide Fabric C strip face up on your sewing machine bed, with a short end toward you. Top it with one of the BBA blocks, face down, aligned at the right, with the longest Fabric B strip at the top (illu. 6-7a). Stitch the two layers together at the right, butting in new BBA blocks until all eight have been added (6-7a). Cut them apart across the strip, as shown in illu. 6-7a. Press the blocks open. The BBAC blocks formed will look like 6-7b.

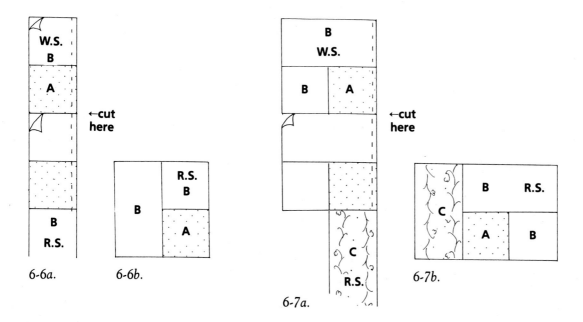

6-6a.　　6-6b.

6-7a.　　6-7b.

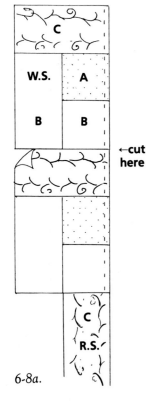

6-8a.

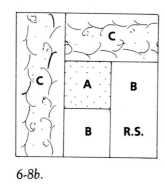

6-8b.

5. Position a 2½-inch-wide Fabric C strip face up on your sewing machine bed, with a short end toward you. Lay one of your BBAC blocks face down over it, with the Fabric C strip to the top, and sew them together at the right, butting in new BBAC blocks until all eight have been added (illu. 6-8a). Take a second strip when needed. Cut them apart across the strip as shown in illu. 6-8a. Press the BBACC blocks formed open. They will look like 6-8b.

6. Set a 2½-inch-wide Fabric D strip face up on your sewing machine bed, with a short end toward you. Top it with one of the BBACC blocks, face down, with the blocks aligned so that the longest C strip is at the top (illu. 6-9) and the right edge of the block aligns with the right edge of the strip. Stitch them together at the right, butting in new BBACC blocks until all eight have been added (illu. 6-9a). Take a second strip when needed. Cut them apart across the strip as shown in 6-9a, and press the blocks open. The BBACCD blocks formed will look like 6-9b. It should be about 9 × 9 inches (including seam allowances).

7. Set a 2½-inch-wide Fabric D strip face up on your sewing machine bed with a short end toward you. Top it with a BBACCD block, with right edges aligned,

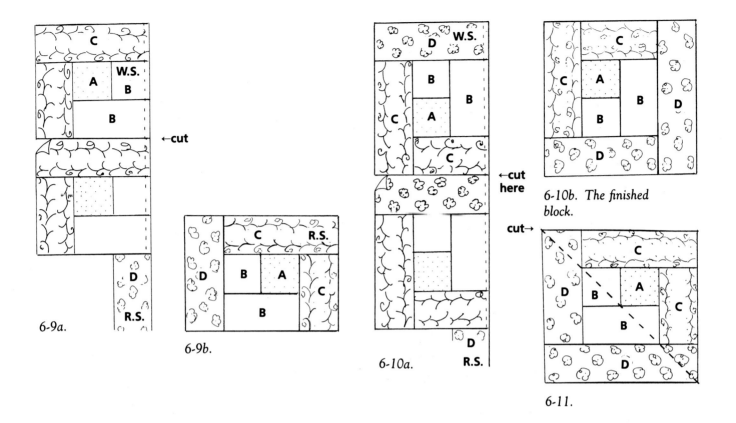

6-9a.

6-9b.

6-10a.

6-10b. *The finished block.*

6-11.

positioned as shown in 6-10a. Stitch them together at the right, butting in new BBACCD blocks until all eight have been added. Take a second strip as needed. Cut them apart across the strip as shown in 6-10a, and press the blocks open. They will look like 6-10b. From these blocks we will make up the Log Cabin triangles (like 6-4) set around the corners of the large red square. The block shown in 6-10b is the traditional Log Cabin block, except that in a traditional block there would be equal strips of light and dark. Press your eight blocks open. Study the photo and carefully cut four of them on the diagonal to make half-block triangles, as shown in illu. 6-11. The C strips should be on only one side of the cut.

8. There are four Log Cabin triangles around the large red center square:

The upper left and lower right triangles. The upper left and lower right triangles have many C strips (green in the model). Each of these triangles is assembled as shown in illu. 6-12, from one pieced block and the two half-block triangles that you just cut—the ones that have the C strips. Sew the two triangles and block together to make a large triangle; make another the same way. Attach one to the upper left and one to the lower right of the bordered red square you made in Step 1 (see illu. 6-14).

The lower left and upper right triangles. You need to make 2 other Log Cabin triangles to go to the lower left and upper right of the large red square. Take 2 of the remaining half-block triangles and a pieced block (from Step 7), and make a large pieced triangle, as shown in illu. 6-13. Make another Log Cabin triangle the same way. Sew one of these Log Cabin triangles to the lower left and one to the upper right of the red square (illu. 6-14).

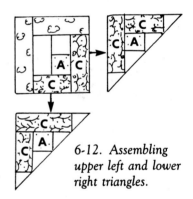

6-12. *Assembling upper left and lower right triangles.*

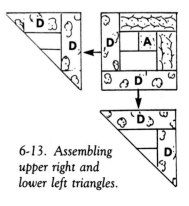

6-13. *Assembling upper right and lower left triangles.*

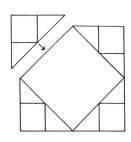

6-14. Sewing a triangle
to the central square.

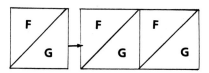

6-15. Joining triangle squares to
make Sawtooth Bars.

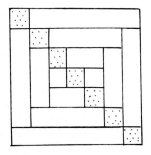

6-16. A Courthouse
Square block.

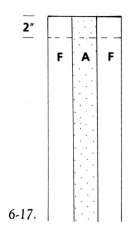

2″

| F | A | F |

6-17.

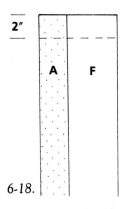

2″

| A | F |

6-18.

Sawtooth Bars Border

9. Next we'll make the Sawtooth Bars borders that go around the pieced square we just completed. In the "Speed Techniques" chapter, read about triangle squares. Take your two 10 × 45 inch rectangles, one of Fabric F and one of Fabric G. On the wrong side of the lighter one, draw a grid of 2⅞-inch squares. Make the grid 13 squares across and 3 down. Draw the diagonals and ¼″ seam allowances around them. Place the two fabrics with right sides facing and sew and cut them into half-triangle squares (see the "Speed Techniques" chapter for details). You'll need 64 squares for your border. Then sew the triangle squares together to form two pieced border strips containing 15 triangle squares each and two pieced border strips containing 17 triangles each (illu. 6-15). Sew the border strips of 17 squares to the top and bottom of the central pieced square you completed in Step 8. (See the border instructions in the "Speed Techniques" chapter.) Sew the strips of 15 pieced squares to the sides of the same square. (You will have extra triangle squares, in case you need them to finish the border, or to use later in a sampler quilt.)

10. Sew a second inside border of 3-inch-wide Fabric A strips to the Sawtooth Bars border. Press the unit and set it aside.

Courthouse Steps Blocks

11. Next, we'll make the Courthouse Steps outer blocks (white and red in model); see illu. 6-16. We'll start from the inside of each block and work out, using speed-piecing techniques. First, join three 2-inch-wide strips on their long sides, in the order of FAF (see illu. 6-17). Measure down 2″ from the top and cut across all 3 strips to make 2″ FAF pieces—keep cutting to make 20 in all. Press them and set them aside.

12. Sew together on a long side a 2-inch-wide Fabric A strip and a 3½-inch wide Fabric F strip. Join another A and F strip of the same sizes in the same way. Cut across both strips to make a 2″ AF unit, as shown in illu. 6-18. Cut a total of 40 of these AF pieces; 2 for each block.

13. Sew one AF piece from Step 12 above an FAF piece from Step 11 and one below it (see illu. 6-19). This will be the center of the Courthouse Square. Make a total of 20 of these centers.

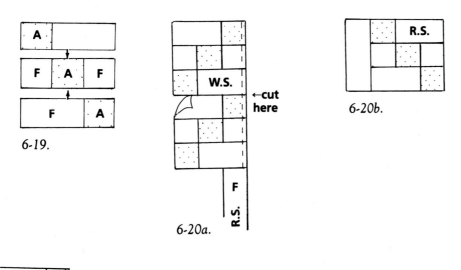

6-19.

6-20a.

6-20b.

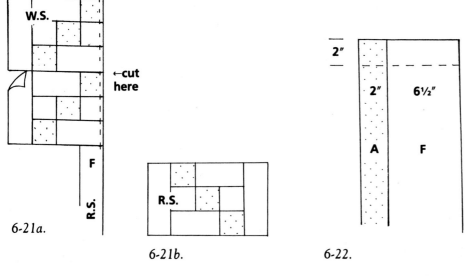

6-21a.

6-21b.

6-22.

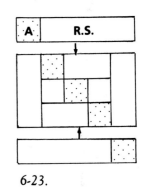

6-23.

14. Place a 2-inch-wide Fabric F strip face up on your sewing machine bed with a short end towards you. Place one completed center from Step 13 face down over it, aligned at the top and the right as shown in illu. 6-20a. Sew them together at the right, butting in other centers; take other 2-inch-wide F strips when needed until all 20 centers have been sewn to a strip. Cut across the strip to separate the units, as shown in illu. 6-20a. Press the units open. They will look like illu. 6-20b.

15. Take a 2-inch-wide F strip. Place it face up on the sewing machine bed with a short end toward you. Place a unit cut in Step 14 over it, face down, aligned at the top and the right as shown in illu. 6-21a. Sew and cut the units apart as you did in the previous step to make 20 units like illu. 6-21b.

16. Sew a 2-inch-wide Fabric A strip to a 6½-inch-wide Fabric F strip on one long side. Make another 2-strip unit the same way. Cut across both strips to make 2″ units as shown in illu. 6-22. Cut 40 of these units. Position one of these units to the top and one to the bottom of the block pieced in Step 15, being sure that the diagonal line of Fabric A squares is continued (see illu. 6-23), and join the units to the block. Repeat for all 20 blocks, and press them.

17. Place a 2-inch-wide Fabric F strip face up, with a short end toward you. Place a block made in Step 16 face down over it, aligned at the top and right side as shown in illu. 6-24a. Sew them together at the right with ¼-inch seam allowances. Butt in another block from Step 16, sew it in the same way, and continue adding blocks to the F strip (about 5 will fit). Take more F strips and continue attaching all the blocks from Step 22 to the strips, until all 20 are attached. Cut them apart across the strip as shown in 6-24a. Press the units open. They will look like 6-24b.

18. In a similar manner, attach each block cut in Step 17 to a 2-inch wide F strip with right sides facing (illu. 6-25a). Cut the blocks apart a shown in illu. 6-25a, and press the units open. They will look like illu. 6-25b. Set them aside.

19. Sew a 2-inch-wide Fabric A strip to a 9½-inch wide Fabric F strip on one side. Repeat one more time. Cut across both strips to make a 2″ pieced strip (see illu. 6-26). Repeat to make a total 40 pieced strips. Press the strips open.

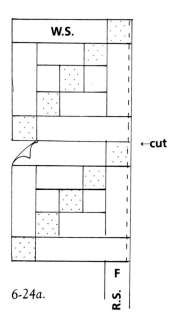

6-24a.

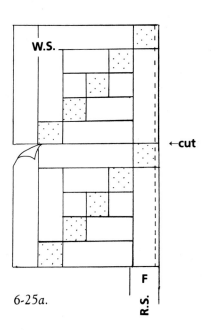

6-25a.

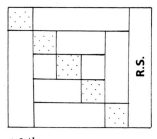

6-24b.

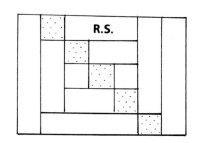

6-25b.

20. Take a block made in Step 18, and two of the strips just pieced in Step 19. Referring to illu. 6-27, sew a strip to the top and one to the bottom of the block, being sure the Fabric A squares continue the diagonal line in the block. This is the completed Courthouse Square block. Repeat the process for each remaining block. You should have a total of 20.

21. Referring to the construction diagram (illu. 6-1), lay out your center pieced square, which you set aside in Step 10, with the Courthouse Square blocks around it. Make a row of the top four central Courthouse Square blocks and then sew the row to the top of the center pieced square. Make a row of the bottom four central Courthouse Square blocks and then sew the row to the bottom of the center pieced square. Make a column of the six Courthouse Square blocks for the left side of the quilt top by sewing them together. Then sew the column to the left side of the center pieced square + Courthouse rows you just joined. Sew together the six Courthouse Square blocks for the right column of the quilt top. Sew it to the right side of the center pieced square + Courthouse rows you just joined (illu. 6-28).

22. Read the section on adding borders in the "Speed Techniques" chapter. Piece your borders from Fabric G and Fabric A, and sew them to the quilt top. Finish the quilt as you like.

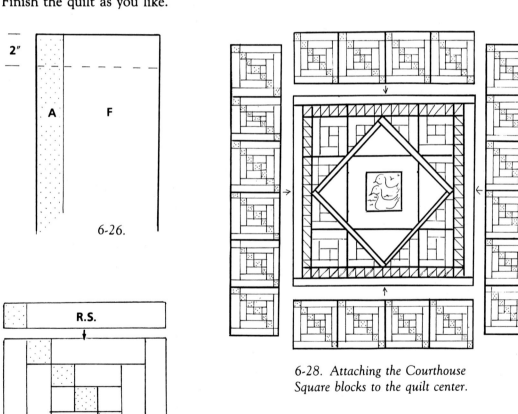

6-28. *Attaching the Courthouse Square blocks to the quilt center.*

6-26.

R.S.

6-27.

7. Wagon Tracks

I was in an antique shop a while back and came across a wonderful quilt. When I went back two days later it was gone—isn't that the way it always is? The design was like that of an Irish Chain or Wagon Tracks, but the center was really made of a nine-patch block, which neither have. The main design of the quilt was the checkerboard pattern. The quilter's skill could be seen in the overall composition. The color was alive even though this quilt was dated 1884. The stitching was masterfully carried out. Well, enough about a treasure that was almost mine—let's go about making a treasure of our own, which is based on my lost treasure. Approximate time to complete the quilt top, 12 hours; fairly easy. The quilt center is made of 12 pieced and 12 unpieced blocks (some of which are cut up); see illu. 7-1. One of the fun things about this pattern is that if you decide to make 24 patchwork blocks, instead of 12 patchwork blocks and 12 solid blocks, you will end up with a different pattern when it is laid out. (My "solid" blocks were printed floral squares with borders printed on them.) Finished size of quilt: 64 × 79 inches. Finished block size: 10½ × 10½ inches (without seam allowances).

YARDAGE*

- 1½ yards of Fabric A (small tan floral print)
- 1¾ yards of Fabric B (off white)
- 1½ yards of Fabric C (large printed floral squares)
- 1½ yards of Fabric D, for solid (outer) border (very light tan)
- 5 yards of fabric for backing
- 5 yards of batting (45 inches wide) or equivalent
- 1 yard of fabric to cut single-thickness bias strips, or 1½ yards to cut double-thickness bias strips

*Colors in parentheses are the colors in the model. Use whatever colors are pleasing to you.

CUTTING

- Twenty-four 2 × 45 inch strips of Fabric A
- Fourteen 2 ×45 inch strips of Fabric B
- Two 5 × 45 inch strips of Fabric B
- Four 3½ × 45 inch strips of Fabric B
- Six 11 inch squares of Fabric C
- Three 11⅜ inch squares of Fabric C; cut these on one diagonal to form 6 triangles for the sides.
- One 11⅞ inch square of Fabric C; cut this on the diagonal in both directions, to form 4 triangles for the corners of the quilt center.
- Eight 5 × 45 inch strips for the solid (outer) border

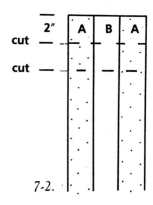

7-2.

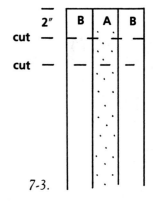

7-3.

7-1. *Construction diagram, Wagon Tracks.*

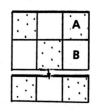

7-4a: *For block center.*

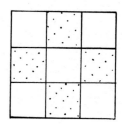

7-4b: *For corners of border.*

• Binding: See binding directions in the "Speed Techniques" chapter to cut binding.

DIRECTIONS

All construction is done with right sides of fabric together and ¼-inch seam allowances.

Making the Pieced Blocks

1. Take 2-inch-wide strips, two of Fabric A and one of Fabric B, and sew them together on one long side in order ABA as shown in illu. 7-2. Join three more strips in the same way. Slice across the 3 strips to make 2-inch pieces (see 7-2). You will need 24 such ABA pieces for the block centers, plus four for the border corners, so make 28 in all.

2. Take 2-inch-wide strips, two of Fabric B and one of Fabric A. Sew them together on one long side in order BAB as shown in illu. 3.

3. Slice them into 2-inch pieces across all 3 strips. You will need 12 BAB pieces for the block centers, plus 8 for the border corners, so make 20 in all. Take two ABA pieces made in Step 1, and sew one to the top and one to the bottom

Wagon Tracks

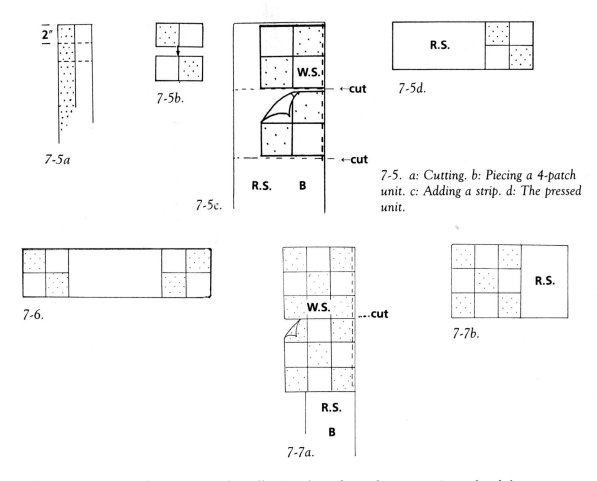

7-5. a: Cutting. b: Piecing a 4-patch unit. c: Adding a strip. d: The pressed unit.

of a BAB piece made in Step 2 (see illu. 7-4a) to form the center 9-patch of the pieced block. Make twelve 9-patches like illu. 7-4a in all. For the border corners, make four 9-patches like 7-4b. Set them aside for now.

4. To make the 4-patch units for the pieced block corners, take a 2-inch-wide strip of Fabric A and a 2-inch-wide strip of Fabric B. Sew them together on one long side. Make four more AB strips. Measure 2″ down and cut across both strips to make 2-inch AB units (7-5a). You will need 96 AB units (8 for each pieced block). Sew them into 4-patch units (7-5b); you'll need a total of forty-eight 4-patch units. Press them; set 24 aside.

5. Place a 5-inch-wide Fabric B strip face up on your sewing machine bed with a short end towards you. Lay a four-patch unit from Step 4 face down over it, aligned at the top and right as shown in 7-5c, and stitch them together at the right. Sew the rest of the twenty-four 4-patch units to a Fabric B strip in the same way (take a second Fabric B strip when the first one is full). Cut across the strip (illu. 7-5c), press the units open (7-5d), and set them aside.

6. Take the twenty-four 4-patch units you set aside in Step 4. Attach one to the Fabric B end of each of the units you made in Step 5 (see illu. 7-6). These will become the top and bottom rows of the pieced blocks.

7. Place a 3½-inch-wide Fabric B strip face up on your sewing machine bed, with a short end toward you. Take your 12 nine-patch block centers (from Step 3). Lay a nine-patch block center over the B strip face down, aligned at the top

65

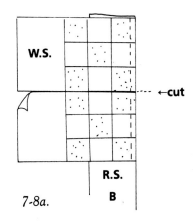

7-8a.

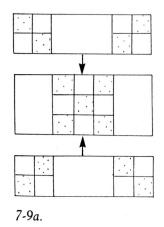

7-9a.

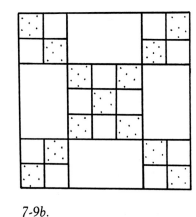

7-9b.

7-8b.

and right, and stitch them together as shown in illu. 7-7a. Continue to sew nine-patch block centers to the strip; take a second Fabric B strip when the first one is full, until all 12 are attached. Cut them apart across the strip and press the units open (7-7b).

8. Place another 3½-inch-wide Fabric B strip face up on your sewing machine bed with a short end toward you. Top it with a unit from Step 7, face down, with the nine-patch positioned as shown in illu. 7-8a. Align the pieces at top and right and stitch the block to the strip as shown in 7-8a. Repeat to sew all the units made in Step 7 to a 3½-inch-wide Fabric B strip; take a second strip when necessary. Press the units open (7-8b).

9. Join two of the units made in Step 6 and one of the units made in Step 8, as shown in illu. 7-9a, to make the finished pieced block (7-9b). Repeat to make all 12 pieced blocks.

Assembling the Quilt Center

10. Study illu. 7-10. You'll see the quilt center is assembled in four rows, set on the diagonal, plus two corner units. Follow illu. 7-10 to pin together the rows and corner units; lay them out on your work surface to be sure everything is positioned correctly. Then sew together the blocks and triangles to make the rows and corner units. After you have pieced together each, sew the corner unit to Row 1; then sew in Row 2, etc., until you have sewn together all the units for the quilt center. Press it and set it aside.

Making the Pieced (Inner) Borders

11. Take two 2-inch-wide strips of Fabric A and sew them together on a short side. Join three more pairs of 2-inch-wide Fabric A strips the same way.

12. Join two 2-inch-wide strips of Fabric B on a short side; repeat for three more pairs of Fabric B.

13. Sew together three 90-inch-long, 2-inch-wide strips from Steps 11 and 12

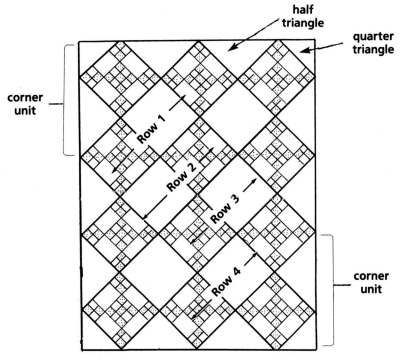

half triangle

quarter triangle

corner unit

Row 1

Row 2

Row 3

Row 4

corner unit

7-10. *Assembly of rows and corners.*

on their long sides in order: A+B+A. Make three more A+B+A pieces the same way.

14. Measure the length of one long side of the pieced quilt center made in Step 10. Cut a 3-strip piece from Step 13 to the same length as the quilt center side; it will be the side pieced border. Attach it to the side of the quilt center. Make and attach the other side pieced border the same way.

15. Measure across the top of the quilt center, not including the side border widths. Cut a 3-strip piece from Step 13 to the same size as the width of the quilt center; it will be the top pieced border. Attach a nine-patch border corner (made in Step 3) to each short end of the top pieced border (illu. 7-11). Make the bottom pieced border in the same way. Then attach the top and bottom pieced borders to the quilt top.

16. For the outer border, use the 5-inch-wide outer border strips. Piece them on a short side, trim them to the length you need, and attach them; see the section on adding borders in the "Speed Techniques" chapter for details. This completes the quilt top.

17. Finish the quilt as you like.

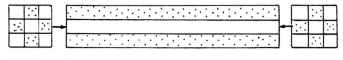

7-11.

8-1. Construction diagram, Nancy's Windmill. Heavy lines are block divisions.

8. Nancy's Windmill

During the 1930s, the Depression had a strong hold on the United States. The U.S. government started a program called the Works Progress Administration (WPA), which provided jobs and encouragement to unemployed people. One part of the WPA, the Arts Projects, aided people who did quilting, weaving, painting, and other arts and crafts. Through the program, many artisans and artists were able to make a living. With the renewed interest in quilting came the need for patterns. The local newspapers came to the rescue by means of syndicated columns that contained quilt patterns. Most of the writers were anonymous or used pen names, like Grandmother Clark, Alice Brooks, or Nancy Page (one of my favorites).

"Nancy Page" was an exception to the anonymity; the writer's identity was given in a byline. She was an Ohio home economist named Florence La Ganke Harris. Her articles were written in the third person, in the setting of a quilting club meeting. Besides Nancy, the club contained three regular members, and the flow of helpful hints seemed endless.

Her patterns started the trend of using flowers in quilts that had not been commonly used before, such as tiger lilies, iris, and pansies. She also came up with many geometric blocks that were beautiful both in their form and in the color choices she suggested for them. Whenever possible, Nancy would tell a little about the history of the pattern—maybe that's why I like her column so much. The pattern that follows has been revised so that speed-piecing can be used. But when the blocks are completed, they are similar to the blocks that Nancy designed. The quilt center is made of 6 rows with 4 blocks in each row. Approximate time to complete the quilt top, 10 to 12 hours; easy. Quilt size: 68 × 89 inches. Finished block size: 11 × 11 inches without seam allowances (see construction diagram, illu. 8-1).

YARDAGE*
- 2 yards of Fabric A for the blocks (red-and-black print)
- 2 yards of Fabric B for the blocks (white and dark red print)
- ¾ yards Fabric A for the first border (red-and-black print)
- 1½ yards of Fabric A for the third border (red-and-black print)
- 1 yard of Fabric C for the second border (solid white)
- 5 yards of fabric for backing.
- 5 yards of batting (45 inches wide) or equivalent
- 1 yard of fabric to cut single-thickness bias binding or 1½ yards of fabric to cut double-thickness bias binding

*Colors given in parentheses are the colors in the model. Use whatever colors are pleasing to you.

CUTTING
- Eight 3½ × 45-inch strips of Fabric A
- Eight 3½ × 45-inch strips of Fabric B
- 30 × 45-inch piece of Fabric A
- 30 × 45-inch piece of Fabric B
- Eight 3 × 45-inch strips of Fabric A for the inner border
- Eight 4 × 45-inch strips of Fabric C for the middle border
- Eight 6 × 45-inch strips of Fabric A for the outer border
- Backing: cut the 5 yards into two 2½-yard-long pieces. Seam them together to make a 90 × 90 inch backing.
- Binding: cut it 4 inches wide for single-thickness bias binding or 6 inches wide for double-thickness bias binding (see "Speed Techniques" chapter for information on binding)

Nancy's Windmill

DIRECTIONS

All construction is done with right sides of fabric facing and ¼-inch seam allowances.

1. Pair off a 3½-inch-wide Fabric A strip with a 3½-inch-wide Fabric B strip. Sew them together on one long side. Make a total of eight AB strip units the same way. Press them open. Measure down 3½ inches from the top and cut across both strips to form an AB piece (illu. 8-2). Keep cutting AB pieces from the AB strip units until you have made 96 AB strips.

2. Next, sew two AB strips (from Step 1) together so the square formed will look like illu. 8-3. Press the unit open, and cut the square on the diagonal as shown in illu. 8-4. Set aside the triangles formed to be used in Step 5.

3. See the directions for triangle squares in the "Speed Techniques" chapter. Take the 30 × 45 inch pieces of Fabric A and Fabric B. On the wrong side of the lighter fabric, draw out a grid of 4⅞-inch squares. You'll need a grid of 48 squares. Mark the diagonal on each square and sew on either side of the diagonal with ¼-inch seam allowances (see illu. 8-5). Cut the units apart on the drawn square and diagonal lines, and press the units open. After all the sewing and cutting is done, you'll end up with 96 triangle squares like 8-5b.

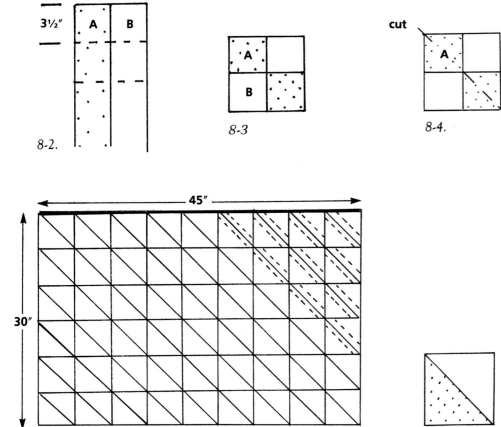

8-2.

8-3.

8-4.

8-5a.

8-5b.

4. Take two triangle squares and sew them together as a row of two squares, as shown in illu. 8-6. Make a total of 48 rows the same way. Then take two of the rows and sew them together to form the windmill square, as shown in illu. 8-7. Make a total of 25 windmill squares.

5. Now you are ready to finish the blocks. Sew one pieced triangle from Step 2 onto each of the four sides of your windmill square (illu. 8-8). If you sew on a triangle and then work your way around the windmill square to attach the other triangles, tucking the seam allowances towards the center as you work, your pieced block will lie well. With all 4 triangles added, the block will look like illu. 8-9. Keep adding pieced triangles to windmill squares to make all 24 blocks. Press them.

6. Lay out the blocks in rows on your work surface, 4 blocks across and 6 rows down (see illu. 8-1 for reference). Sew the blocks together in rows. Then sew the rows together to make the quilt center.

7. Read the section on adding borders in the "Speed Techniques" chapter. Piece the inner border strips, trim the borders to the correct size for your quilt center, and add the border. Repeat for the middle and outer border.

8. Finish the quilt as you like. Since the piecing pattern is busy, stitching in the ditch or outline quilting might be a good choice of quilting pattern. This is also a good pattern to tie.

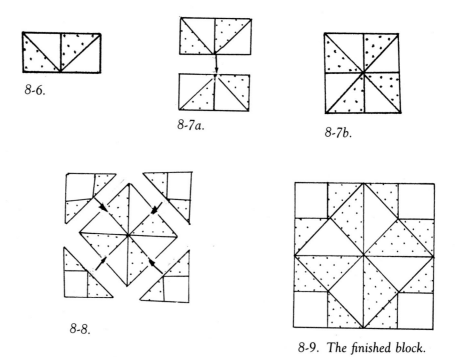

8-6.

8-7a.

8-7b.

8-8.

8-9. The finished block.

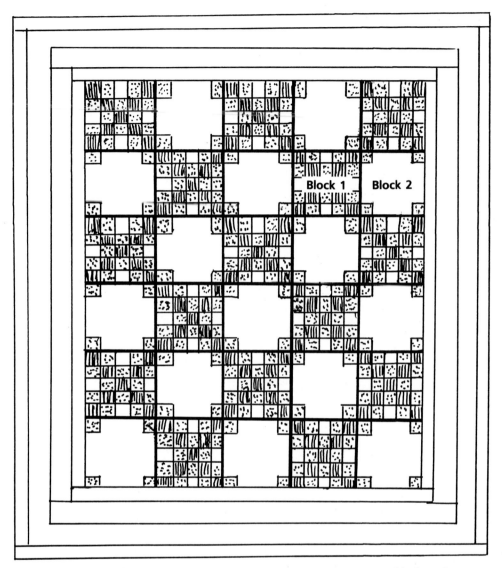

9-1. *Construction diagram, Double Irish Chain. Dark lines are block outlines.*

9. Double Irish Chain

The Double Irish Chain was very popular around the mid-1700s. We can be fairly confident of the date by a study of the fabrics used and from written records. While rather simple, it is nonetheless beautiful; we admire it today as much as they did some 240 years ago.

The pattern given here is made up of 30 blocks, 15 in each of two designs which are alternated to make up the pattern (see the construction diagram, illu. 9-1). The border yardages are given separately, in case you don't want to repeat the colors of your central design in the border. Approximate time to piece the quilt top, 10 hours; easy. Quilt size: 72 × 82 inches; finished block size (not including seam allowances) 10 × 10 inches.

Double Irish Chain

YARDAGE*

- 1 yard of Fabric A for the blocks (red print)
- 1¾ yards of Fabric A for the second and fourth borders (red print)
- 1½ yards of Fabric B for the blocks (white-and-black print)
- ⅔ yard of Fabric B for the inner border (white-and-black print)
- 1½ yards of Fabric C for the blocks (off white)
- 1 yard of Fabric C for the third border (off white)
- 5 yards of fabric for backing
- 5 yards of batting
- 1 yard of fabric to cut single-thickness bias binding or 1½ yards to cut double-thickness bias binding

*Colors in parentheses are the colors in the model. Choose whatever colors are pleasing to you.

CUTTING

- Ten 2½ × 45 inch strips of Fabric A (for blocks)
- Eighteen 2½ × 45 inch strips of Fabric B (for blocks)
- Four 2½ × 45 inch strips of Fabric C (for blocks)
- Six 6½ × 45 inch strips of Fabric C (for blocks)
- Eight 2½ × 45 inch strips of Fabric B (for the inner border)
- Eight 4 × 45 inch strips of Fabric A (for the second border)
- Eight 4 × 45 inch strips of Fabric C (for the third border)
- Eight 2½ × 45 inch strips of Fabric A (for the fourth border)
- Backing: Cut the backing into two 2½-yard lengths and seam them together on a long side to make a 90 × 90 inch piece
- Binding: 4 inches wide for single-thickness bias binding; 6 inches wide for double-thickness bias binding (see "Speed Techniques" chapter section on binding)

DIRECTIONS

All piecing is done with right sides of fabric facing and ¼-inch seam allowances.

1. To make the blocks, we'll first sew our 2½-inch-wide strips lengthwise into sheets. Sew the first sheet of strips in the order A+B+C+B+A. Make a second sheet the same way. Press it, and measure down from the top 2½ inches; cut across all the strips to make an ABCBA row (see illu. 9-2). Continue cutting to make a total of 30 of these rows. Label these pieces as being from Step 1 and set them aside.

2. To make our next set of sheets, take 2½-inch-wide strips and sew them lengthwise in the order B+A+B+A+B. Make two sheets in this order. Press them. Measure down from the top 2½ inches; cut across all the strips to make a BABAB row (see illu. 9-3). Continue cutting to make a total of 30 of these rows. Label them as being from Step 2 and set them aside.

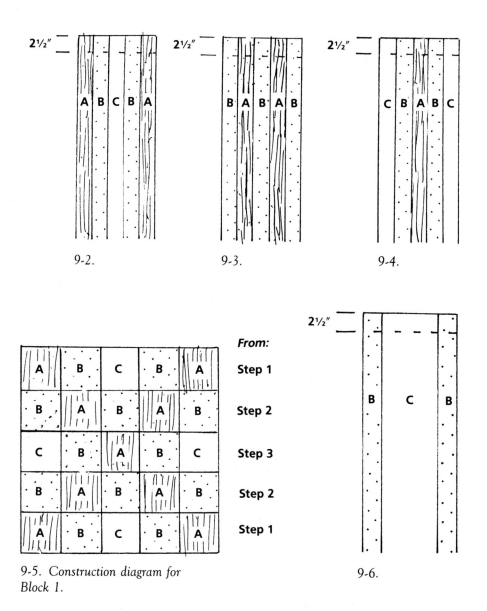

2½″ ABCBA 9-2.

2½″ BABAB 9-3.

2½″ CBABC 9-4.

9-5. Construction diagram for
Block 1.

	From:
A B C B A	Step 1
B A B A B	Step 2
C B A B C	Step 3
B A B A B	Step 2
A B C B A	Step 1

2½″ B C B 9-6.

3. Make one sheet of 2½-inch-wide strips by sewing them lengthwise in the order C+B+A+B+C (see illu. 9-4). Press the sheet; measure down from the top 2½ inches and cut across all the strips to make a CBABC row. Cut a total of 15 of these rows. Label them as being from Step 3 and set them aside.

4. Take a good look at illu. 9-5, the block piecing diagram. This is how all the Block 1 blocks of the quilt should look when they are pieced. The block is made by joining five rows (cut in steps 1, 2, and 3). For each block you need two ABCBA rows (from Step 1), two BABAB rows (from Step 2), and one CBABC row from Step 3. Sew the rows together on a long side in the order shown in illu. 10-5 until you have pieced the entire block. Make a total of 15 Block 1 blocks the same way. Press them and set them aside.

5. Make a sheet of strips by sewing them together on their long side as follows: a 2½-inch-wide Fabric B strip + a 6½-inch-wide Fabric C strip + a 2½-inch-wide Fabric B strip. Make another sheet the same way. Press them; measure down 2½

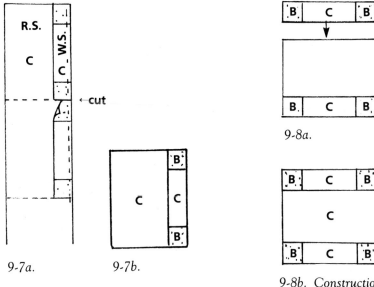

9-8a.

9-7a.   9-7b.

9-8b. *Construction diagram for Block 2.*

inches from the top of the sheet and cut across all the strips (illu. 9-6). Make a total of 30 of these BCB rows (2 for each Block 2 block). Set 15 aside.

6. Place a 6½-inch-wide Fabric C strip face up on your sewing machine bed, with the short side towards you. Lay a BCB row (from Step 5) face down over it, aligned as shown in illu. 9-7a. Sew them together at the right. Butt in new BCB rows along the strip, taking new 6½-inch-wide Fabric C strips when needed, until fifteen BCB rows have been attached to the strips. Cut the units apart across the strip as shown in illu. 9-7a to separate the units. Press them open. They will look like 9-7b.

7. Working with a pieced unit from Step 6, take one of the 15 BCB rows set aside in Step 5, and sew it to the Fabric C side of the pieced unit (see ill. 9-8a). This makes a Block 2 block; illu. 9-8b shows what your completed Block 2 looks like. Make a total of fifteen Block 2 blocks the same way.

8. Lay out the fifteen Block 1 blocks and the fifteen Block 2 blocks on your work surface; see illu. 9-1 for reference. Next, sew the blocks for each row (across) together as follows:

Row 1: Block 1 + Block 2 + Block 1 + Block 2 + Block 1
Row 2: Block 2 + Block 1 + Block 2 + Block 1 + Block 2
Row 3: Block 1 + Block 2 + Block 1 + Block 2 + Block 1
Row 4: Block 2 + Block 1 + Block 2 + Block 1 + Block 2
Row 5: Block 1 + Block 2 + Block 1 + Block 2 + Block 1
Row 6: Block 2 + Block 1 + Block 2 + Block 1 + Block 2

As you can see, the blocks alternate left to right as well as up and down.

9. After sewing the blocks into rows, sew the rows together to complete the center of the quilt top. Then read in the "Speed Techniques" chapter about adding borders. Add the borders and finish the quilt as you like. (The large open areas in the Block 2 blocks are a wonderful place for a pretty quilting pattern.)

10. The Queen's Petticoat

This quilt dates from about 1760, a very tumultuous time for the British colonies in North America. Approximate time to complete the quilt top, 12 to 15 hours; fairly easy. Quilt size: 59 × 84 inches. The quilt pieces are cut by speed-cutting methods and assembled into 72 rows of 3 kinds, which are then sewn together (see construction diagram, illu. 10-1, and illu. 10-9).

YARDAGE*

- 1¼ yards of Fabric A (blue)
- 1½ yards of Fabric B (white) for quilt blocks
- ¾ yard of Fabric B (white) for inner border
- ¾ yard of Fabric C (red) for quilt blocks
- 1 yard of Fabric C (red) for outer border
- ½ yard of Fabric D (yellow print)
- 1½ yards of Fabric E (dark green print)
- 1 yard of Fabric F (light green)
- 4 yards of batting (45 inches wide) or equivalent
- 4 yards of fabric for backing
- 1 yard of fabric to cut single-thickness bias binding or 1½ yards to cut double-thickness bias binding

*Colors in parentheses are the colors used in the model. Use whatever colors are pleasing to you. Border yardages are given separately in case you want to change their color.

CUTTING

- Three 2½ × 45 inch strips of Fabric A
- 31 × 21 inch piece of Fabric A
- Six 2½ × 45 inch strips of Fabric B
- 31 × 21 inch piece of Fabric B
- Eight 3 × 45 inch strips of Fabric B (for inner border)
- Nine 2½ × 45 inch strips of Fabric C
- Eight 4 × 45 inch strips of Fabric C (for outer border)
- Six 2½ × 45 inch strips of Fabric D
- Six 2½ × 45 inch strips of Fabric E
- 31 × 21 inch piece of Fabric E
- Binding: See binding directions in the "Speed Techniques" chapter.

The Queen's Petticoat

DIRECTIONS

All construction is done with right sides of fabric facing and ¼-inch seam allowances.

1. Take a 2½-inch-wide Fabric A strip and a 2½-inch-wide Fabric C strip, and sew them together on one long side. Make two more strip pairs the same way. Take one pair, measure down 2½ inches from the top edge, and cut across both strips to form a two-patch AC unit (illu. 10-2). Continue cutting until you have cut 48 two-patch units. Now sew 2 two-patch units together to form a checkerboard (illu. 10-3). You'll need 24 AC checkerboards. Press them and set them aside.

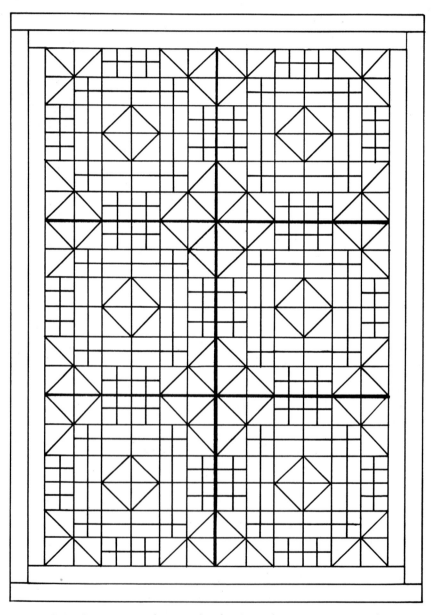

10-1. Construction diagram for the Queen's Petticoat. Heavy lines divide pattern units.

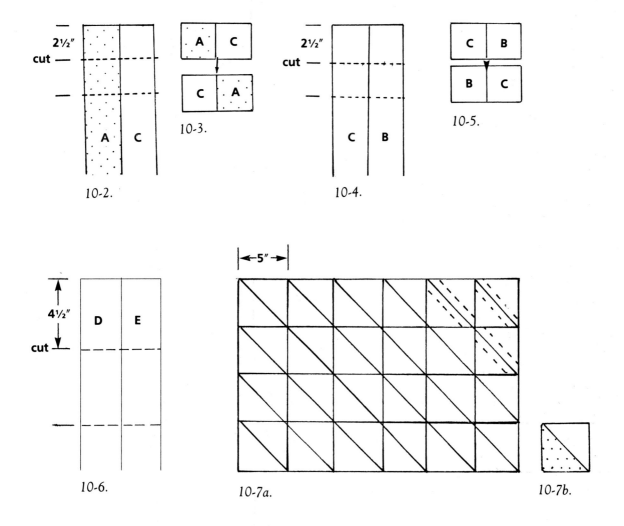

10-3.

10-2.

10-5.

10-4.

10-6.

10-7a.

10-7b.

2. Sew a 2½-inch-wide Fabric C strip to a 2½-inch-wide Fabric B strip on one long side. Make 5 more pairs of strips the same way. Measure down 2½ inches from the top of the unit and cut across both strips (illu. 10-4). Continue cutting pairs of strips into 2-patch CB units; you will need a total of 96. Sew two CB 2-patch units into a checkerboard (see illu. 10-5). You'll need 48 CB checkerboards. Press them and set them aside.

3. Sew a 2½ inch wide Fabric D strip to a 2½ inch wide Fabric E strip on one long side. Make a total of 6 pairs of DE strips. Measure down 4½ inches from the top and cut across both strips (illu. 10-6). Continue until you cut 48 pieces. Press them and set them aside.

4. In the "Speed Techniques" chapter, read about how to make 2-triangle squares. Take your 31 × 21 pieces of Fabric A and Fabric B. On the wrong side of the lighter fabric, draw 4⅞ inch squares, 6 across and 4 down (see 10-7a). Mark the diagonals, stitch ¼-inch away on either side of the diagonals, cut the units apart on the square and diagonal lines, and press the units open. They will look like 10-7b. You will need forty-eight AB 2-triangle squares.

5. Using the 21 × 31 inch pieces of fabrics E and F, make 48 EF 2-triangle squares, in the same way that you made the AB 2-triangle squares in Step 4.

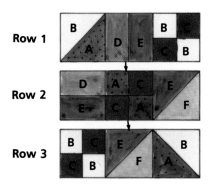

*10-8. Rows that form a block,
positioned as they would be joined.*

6. Next, we will sew our small units together to form rows and then blocks. The first row (Row 1) to our block is made up of pieces sewn in steps 2, 3, and 4. Study illu. 10-8, Row 1. Sew your AB 2-triangle square from Step 4 so it is on the left-hand side of Row 1, with the Fabric B triangle in the upper left-hand corner. Sew the AB 2-triangle square to a DE unit from Step 3, aligned as shown in illu. 10-8. Next, add a CB checkerboard (from Step 2) at the right of Row 1; make sure that the Fabric B squares on the checkerboard are in the upper left and lower right corners (see illu. 10-8). Make a total of 24 of Row 1 in the same way.

7. Row 2 (see illu. 10-8, Row 2) of your block is sewn from pieces made in steps 1, 3, and 5. Place a DE unit from Step 3 horizontally with the Fabric D to the top; sew it to an AC checkerboard from Step 1, aligned so the Fabric A squares of the checkerboard are in the upper left and lower right-hand corners. Add an EF 2-triangle square from Step 5; make sure the Fabric E triangle is in the upper left hand corner. Make a total of 24 of Row 2. Lay out Row 1 and Row 2 as shown in illu. 10-8 and sew the two rows together. Repeat to join all 24 of each row. You're now two-thirds of the way done with your blocks.

8. Row 3 (see illu. 10-8, Row 3) of your block is sewn from units made in steps 2, 4, and 5. Sew a CB checkerboard from Step 3, with the Fabric B squares in the upper left and lower right-hand corner of the checkerboard, to an EF 2-triangle square; make sure the Fabric E triangle is in the upper left-hand corner. Add an AB 2-triangle square from Step 4; make sure the Fabric A triangle is in the lower left-hand corner. Make 24 of Row 3 in the same way. Sew Row 3 to the two-row units you made in Step 7, positioned as shown in illu. 10-8. Repeat for all 24 blocks.

9. Now you're ready to lay out the blocks made in Step 8, for the quilt center. Study illu. 11-9. You'll see that the 3-row blocks are joined in groups of 4 to make six main pattern units. Place an upside down block (Block 1) in the upper left corner of your work surface (see illu. 10-9). To its right, the next block (Block 2) is rotated a quarter turn (90 degrees). Block 3 is rotated a quarter turn from block 2. Block 4 is rotated a quarter turn from Block 3. Pin the 4 blocks together as shown in the upper left of Fig. 10-9 and sew them together to make a pattern unit. Make 5 more pattern units the same way. When they are completed, join them as shown in illu. 10-9 to make the quilt center.

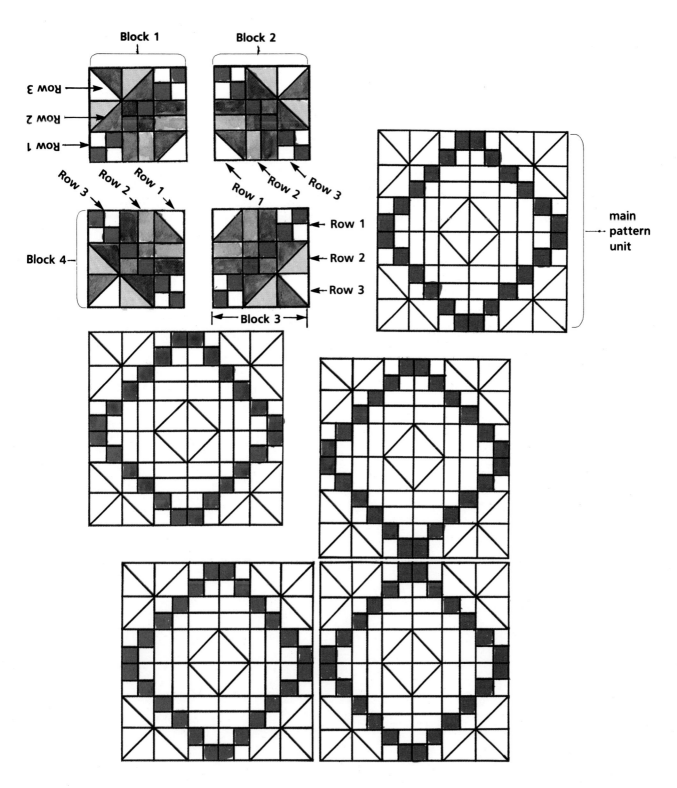

10-9. *Diagram showing orientation of blocks to make up a pattern unit, and pattern units to make up the quilt center.*

10. Read the instructions in the "Speed Techniques" chapter about adding borders. Attach the inner border strips to the quilt center sides. Attach the top and bottom inner border strips across the top and the bottom of the quilt center, including the width of the side inner borders.

11. Attach the outer border strips in the same way as you did the inner border strips.

12. Finish the quilt as you like. Since it is such a busy pattern, a simple quilting pattern, like outline quilting or tying, might be a good choice.

11. Crazy Quilt

Crazy quilts were very popular around 1850. Quilters enjoyed letting their treasures show up in their quilts. My inspiration for the pattern given here was the Botanist's Quilt at the Smithsonian Institution in Washington, D.C., by botanist Augusta E. D. Bussey. Her love of flowers spills out all over her quilt, on which she masterfully embroidered many floral arrangements.

Our present quilt uses machine embroidery and fusible interfacing to attach the pieces to the quilt blocks and quilt the layers at the same time. If you want to make it larger, you can add additional borders. Approximate time to complete the quilt, 2 to 3 weeks; fairly easy. Quilt size: 60 × 73.5 inches. If you want to make it larger, add on extra borders. Finished block size: 12 × 12 inches (without seam allowances).

YARDAGE AND SUPPLIES
- The equivalent of 5 yards of satin scraps, in about 10 colors that go well together.
- About 10 yards of scrap lace in several patterns and about 40 yards of woven ribbon in several patterns, if desired
- 3¼ yards of backing fabric (if fabric is 45 inches wide) or 2½ yards of backing fabric (if fabric is 60 inches wide)
- Fabric glue
- 3 yards (if 45 inches wide) of fusible interfacing with adhesive on one side only, or enough to cut twenty 12½-inch squares
- 5 yards (if 45 inches wide) of batting, or equivalent
- 2¾ yards of velvet (45 inches wide) for borders and joiner strips

CUTTING
- Twenty 5-inch-squares of satin (for center diamonds of blocks)
- Eighty 3-inch squares of satin (for corners of blocks)
- Twenty 15-inch squares of backing fabric
- Twenty 12-inch squares of batting
- Eight 4 × 45 inch strips of batting (for the borders)
- Twenty 12½-inch squares of fusible interfacing
- Eleven 2 × 45 inch velvet strips for making joiner strips
- Eight 8 × 45 inch velvet strips for borders; make sure to cut them on the grain
- Irregular shapes cut from the satin scraps (see color photo for guidance)

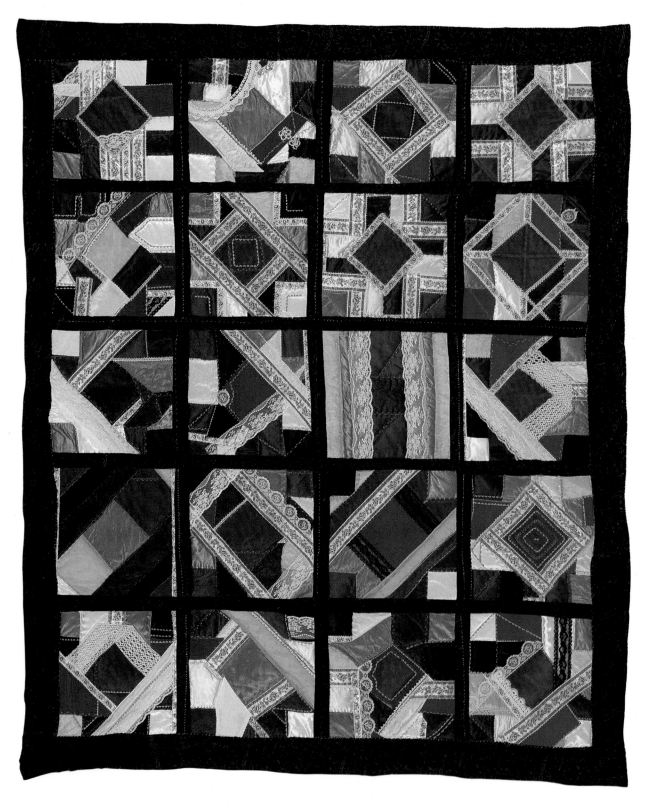

Crazy Quilt

DIRECTIONS

Note: velvet has a nap; it looks different when the fabric is turned upside down than it does right-side up; keep this in mind when piecing. Construction (adding joiner strips, sewing rows together, adding borders) is done with ¼-inch seam allowances and right sides of fabric facing.

1. Our early work is done on the ironing board or other ironing surface. Put a fusible interfacing square (12 × 12 inches) with its adhesive side up on your ironing surface, with the iron set high enough to fuse the interfacing, but low enough to avoid damaging the satin. Press a 3-inch square of satin in each of the corners of the interfacing square (see illu. 11-1). Notice that you were not told to fold under a ¼-inch seam allowance on the squares before pressing: the fabric pieces added later will cover up with their own edges the initial raw edge. Place your 5-inch satin square on point to form a diamond in the center of your interfacing square, and pin it in place, but don't press or sew it down yet.

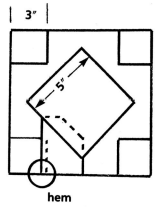

11-1.

2. The next step is to cover the whole surface of each block with a pleasing design of scrap satin, lace, and ribbon. Pin irregular pieces on your interfacing square, folding under a ¼-inch hem where two edges of fabric meet and overlapping the folded fabric over the raw edge of the adjacent fabric (see illu. 11-1). The raw edges of fabric that would extend into the area of the center diamond should be tucked *under* the diamond. The diamond edges may be outlined in lace or ribbon if you wish. Also apply scrap lace and ribbon in other places where it looks appealing; tack it down with a small amount of fabric glue until later. When you have gotten all the pieces where you want them, fuse them to the interfacing. To make sure that the fabric is really secured, you may wish to turn your block over and press it firmly from the back. Continue in this way until all 20 blocks are assembled.

3. Now that all the fabric is placed the way you want it, let's take our 20 blocks to the sewing machine. Lay out a 15-inch backing fabric square with the wrong side up. Center a 12-inch square of batting on the backing square. Finally, center your quilt block, face up, on the batting. Pin the center and the four corners so the layers won't slide around. Using embroidery stitches that are pleasing to you, machine appliqué all edges where fabrics meet. Sew down all the lace also. You can add extra embroidery for decoration if you wish. This will quilt the blocks at the same time. Start your sewing from the center of the block and work outwards. Sew up to ¼ inch away from the block's edges. Continue until all 20 blocks have been sewn in this way. Lay out the blocks in a pleasing design on your work surface, and label them with a bit of tape with the block number and the direction of the top of the block (11-2).

4. Next we'll be sewing velvet joiner strips to the left of the following blocks: 1, 2, 3, 5, 6, 7, 9, 10, 11, 13, 14, 15, 17, 18, and 19 (see illu. 11-2). Place a 2-inch-wide velvet joiner strip face up on your sewing machine bed. Lay the top right block (#1) over it, face down, with the top of the block at the top of the strip and the layers aligned at right (illu. 11-3). Move both the backing and batting out of the way so they're not sewn in. Sew the strip to the block at the right. Sew each of the remaining 14 blocks listed above to the joiner strips in the same way, taking new joiner strips as necessary. Cut the units apart across the strip (illu. 11-3).

5. Take blocks 1, 2, and 3 and sew these together by attaching a block to the

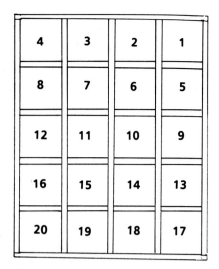

4	3	2	1
8	7	6	5
12	11	10	9
16	15	14	13
20	19	18	17

11-2. *Construction diagram showing block numbers.*

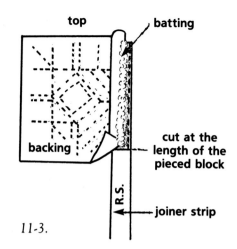

11-3.

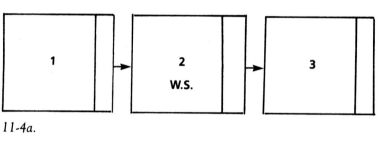

11-4a.

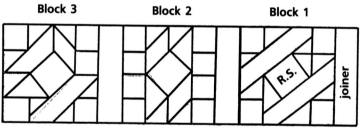

11-4b.

"empty" side of a joiner strip (illu. 11-4a). The row of three blocks will look something like 11-4b. Set it aside. Join the blocks 5-6-7, 9-10-11, 13-14-15, and 17-18-19 in the same way.

6. Attach the fourth (leftmost) block in each row (blocks 4, 8, 12, 16, and 20) to the correct 3-block unit made in Step 5 (see illu. 11-2). When you are done, you will have 5 rows of 4 blocks each, separated by joiner strips.

7. Working on the wrong side of a row, overlap the backing from the far left block onto the adjacent block. Make sure the batting and backing lie flat. Trim off any excess batting. Fold under ¼ inch of the backing's side seam and slipstitch it in place over the next block, starting in ¼ inch from the top of the block, and

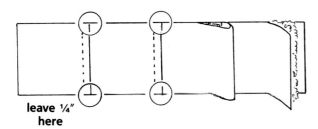

leave ¼″
here

*11-5. Overlap the backing onto the next
block and slipstitch in place.*

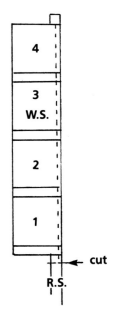

11-6.

stopping ¼ inch away from the block's bottom. Repeat this process until all the side seams of the inside blocks are closed (see illu. 11-5). Repeat with each of the remaining rows in the same way.

8. Sew together the short ends of two 45-inch joiner strips of velvet. Place the 2-strip unit face up on your sewing machine bed. Lay the first row of blocks face down over it with block 4 at the top (11-6). Move both the backing and the batting out of the way on the top block and stitch down the side to attach the joiner strip to the block. Cut off the excess strip that extends beyond the row. Repeat for rows 2, 3, and 4. The highest number of block for that row must always be at the top of the strip to keep your row in position. Any leftover joiner strip can be sewn at its short end to another joiner strip and used for another row.

9. Sew the rows together by attaching the joiner strip below Row 1 to the top of Row 2, etc., moving the backing and batting out of the way as you go. Then trip off any excess batting, fold under a ¼-inch hem on the backing between the rows, overlap the backing from one row to the next, and slipstitch it in place.

10. To make the side borders, take two 8-inch-wide velvet border strips and sew them together on a short end to make an 89.5 inch long strip. Join a total of 4 pairs of strips. (You'll need two border strips for the sides and two for the top and bottom, in the next step.) Join two 4-inch-wide batting strips on their short ends also, and make 3 more pairs of joined batting strips the same way. (You'll need two for the side borders and two for the top and bottom borders, in the next step.) Place an 89.5-inch strip of 4-inch-wide batting on your sewing machine bed, top it with one of the 89.5-inch border strips, face up, and lay your quilt top over it, also face up (see illu. 11-7), all aligned at the top and right. Sew them together at the right with ½-inch seam allowances. When you reach the end of the quilt top, stop. Cut off any excess batting and border strip that extends beyond the quilt top's edge (see illu. 11-7). Repeat the same process to attach the border strip and batting to the opposite side of the quilt top. Trim off any excess batting close to the sewing line to reduce bulk at the seams. Turn the velvet border strips and the batting around to the front of the quilt top, fold under a ¼ inch hem, and pin the borders in place on the front of the quilt top. Sew them in place using a machine embroidery stitch.

11. To attach the top and bottom borders, take the two remaining 89.5-inch-long, 4-inch-wide batting strips you made in Step 10. Take the remaining two 89.5-inch long, 8-inch wide border strips you made in Step 10. For the top border, place the strip of batting on your sewing machine bed. Lay an 8-inch-wide velvet border strip face up over it, with the end of the border strip extending 2 inches beyond the top edge of the batting. Pin the batting and border to the top edge of the quilt top as shown in illu. 11-8 (quilt top over border strip). When you get to the far edge of the quilt top, let the border extend 2 inches beyond the edge of the quilt top; trim off the rest of the border. Also trim off the batting so it doesn't extend beyond the edge of the quilt top. Fold the 2-inch extended pieces of the border to the quilt's front and pin them in place. Trim the seam allowances of the quilt border corners to ease turning of the border later. Stitch down the length of the border to join the top border to the quilt top, as shown in 11-8. When it is attached, turn the top border strip to the front, turn under a hem, and machine stitch the border strip in place, as you did for the side borders. Repeat the same process to attach the bottom border. Quilt the borders as you wish to complete the quilt.

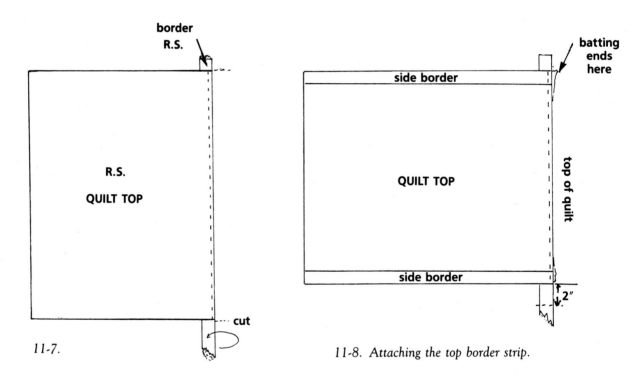

11-7.

11-8. *Attaching the top border strip.*

12. Framed Quilt Center

During the first half of the 19th century, many quilts were made that used a printed quilt center or pillow cover as the center block. The quilt pattern that follows is based on a quilt at the Smithsonian Institution, in Washington, D.C. It was made *between 1815 and 1830 by Mrs. William Alston, who lived on a plantation near Georgetown, South Carolina. In reproducing this quilt, I tried to find fabrics with similar prints. If you see the original, you may wonder how I came up with what I did, because the original is in browns and oranges, but mine is done in greens. Finding fabrics like the old ones was difficult, so I concentrated, basically, on matching print types. I hope you enjoy sewing it as much as I did. Approximate time to complete the quilt top, 6 hours; very easy. Quilt size: 88 × 88 inches.*

YARDAGE*

- Printed 18-inch-square center block**
- Two 12½-inch-square printed center blocks with a pattern that matches the 18-inch block or goes with it
- 1⅔ yards of Fabric A (dark green with small print)
- 1¼ yards of Fabric B (light pink with green print)
- 1 yard of Fabric C (dark green floral print)
- 1¼ yards of Fabric D (pink with red print)
- 1¾ yards of Fabric E (green and red paisley print)
- 5 yards of batting (45 inches wide) or equivalent
- 5 yards of fabric for backing
- 1¼ yards of fabric to cut single-thickness bias binding or 1¾ yards of fabric to cut double-thickness bias binding

*Colors and patterns in parentheses are those of the model. Choose whatever fabrics are pleasing to you.

** If you can't find an 18-inch-square printed center block, buy a 12½-inch square one instead, and add a 3½-inch border around it (the finished border width will be 3 inches), which will make it 18 × 18. Use it to replace the 18-inch square.

CUTTING

- Cut two 12½-inch printed blocks in half on the diagonal to form a total of 4 triangles
- Four 3 × 45 inch strips of Fabric A (for border 1)
- Eight 5 × 45 inch strips of Fabric A (for border 10)
- Ten 4 × 45 inch strips of Fabric B (for border 2 and border 6)
- Ten 3 × 45 inch strips of Fabric C (for border 3 and border 7)
- Five 5 × 45 inch strips of Fabric D (for border 4)
- Seven 2 × 45 inch strips of Fabric D (for border 8)
- Thirteen 4 × 45 inch strips of Fabric E (for border 5 and border 9)
- Backing: Cut it into two 2½-yard pieces and seam them together on one long side to make a 90 × 90 inch pieced backing.
- Bias binding: Cut 4″ inches wide for single-thickness bias binding or 6 inches wide for double-thickness bias binding.

DIRECTIONS

All construction is done with right sides of fabric facing and ¼-inch seam allowances. See the construction diagram (illu. 12-1) as a reference for all the steps that follow, and read the section on attaching borders in the "Speed Techniques" chapter before starting.

1. Mark the center of the cut (long) edge of your four printed triangles and align the triangle's center with the center of the side of the 18-inch printed square. Pin the two pieces face to face with raw edges aligned and sew the triangle to the square. Sew the three remaining triangles onto the square in the same way (illu. 12-2). Press the unit.

2. Take your four 3-inch-wide Fabric A strips. To attach border 1, stitch one

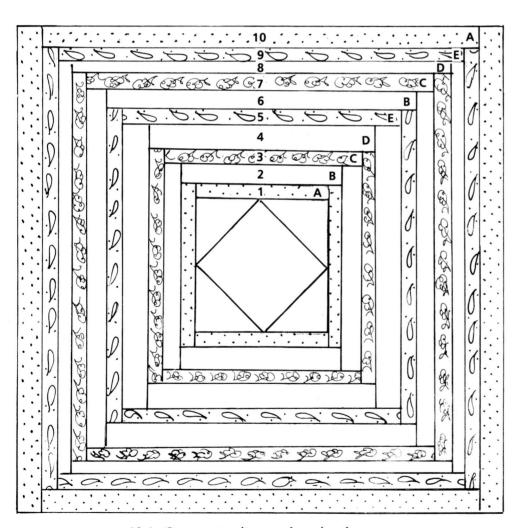

12-1. Construction diagram, framed quilt center.

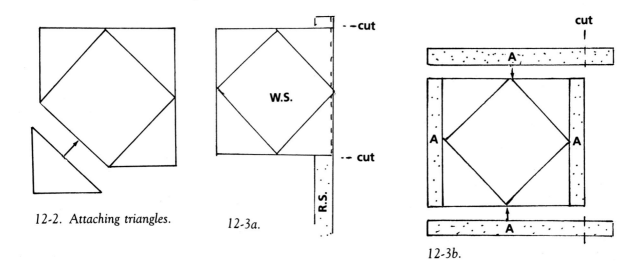

12-2. *Attaching triangles.*

12-3a.

12-3b.

12-3. *a. Attaching side A borders. b. Attaching top and bottom A borders.*

strip to the left side of the quilt center (12-3a); trim off the excess border. Stitch the second strip to the opposite side of the quilt center and trim off the excess. Stitch the third border strip to the top of the quilt center, including the widths of the left and right borders just added (12-3b); trim off the excess border. Stitch the fourth border strip to the bottom of the quilt center in the same way as you did for the top border, and trim off the excess. Press the unit open.

3. To attach border 2, sew the four 4-inch-wide Fabric B borders onto the unit made in Step 2 (illu. 12-4), in the same way you sewed on the Fabric A borders.

4. To attach border 3, sew the four 3-inch-wide Fabric C borders to the unit you made in Step 3, in the same way you sewed on the Fabric A borders.

5. To attach the remaining borders, you will need to piece your border strips, because the borders need to be longer than 45″. Piece the border strips you need to use into a long strip by sewing them together on their short sides. The fabric used for each remaining border is listed below:

Border 3: Four 3-inch-wide strips of Fabric C
Border 4: Five 5-inch-wide strips of Fabric D
Border 5: Five 4-inch-wide strips of Fabric E
Border 6: Six 4-inch-wide strips of Fabric B
Border 7: Six 3-inch-wide strips of Fabric C
Border 8: Seven 2-inch-wide strips of Fabric D
Border 9: Eight 4-inch-wide strips of Fabric E
Border 10: Eight 5-inch-wide strips of Fabric A

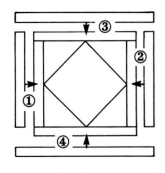

12-4. *Order of attaching all borders.*

6. Finish the quilt as you like. For busy prints, using a simple quilting pattern or tying is a good idea.

13. Overall Bill

Overall Bill and Sunbonnet Sue are two quilt patterns that became popular in the 1920s. They first appeared as friends in a primer. Over the years, Bill and Sue have undergone many changes, appearing sometimes as Dutch dolls, colonial ladies and gents, and modern-day children who play football, basketball, and use computers. Approximate time to complete the quilt top, 10 hours; fairly easy. This is a great pattern for using up those small pieces of favorite fabrics that you have on hand. Quilt size: 56 × 70 inches. Finished block size, 11.5 × 11.5 inches (without seam allowances); has 12 blocks (see illu. 13-1).

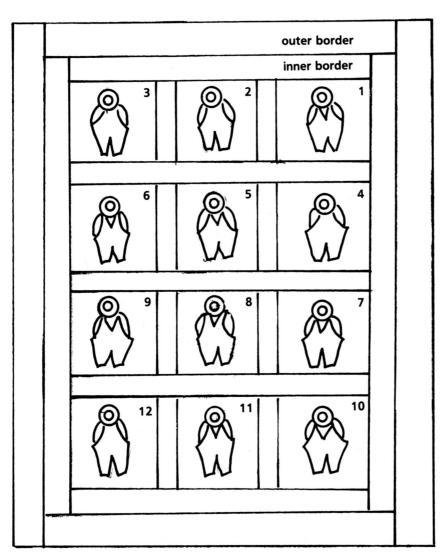

13-1. Construction diagram for Overall Bill.

YARDAGE*

- Scraps of 7 or more fabrics for the overalls; scraps should be at least 6 × 7 inches each; about ½ yard total
- Scraps of 6 or more fabrics for hats and shirts; scraps should be at least 4 × 6 inches each; about ⅔ yard total
- 1½ yards of Fabric A for blocks (off white)
- 1¼ yards of Fabric B for the joiner strips and inner border (blue-green and white print)
- 1 yard of Fabric C for the outer border (solid blue-green)
- 1 yard of fusible interfacing (45 inches wide) or equivalent
- 4 yards of backing
- 4 yards of batting (45 inches wide) or equivalent
- Binding: 1 yard of fabric to cut single-thickness binding; 1¾ yards of fabric to cut double-thickness binding

*Colors in parentheses are the colors in the model. Use whatever colors are pleasing to you.

CUTTING

- Cut a 4-inch-diameter circle and a 2¼-inch diameter circle from cardboard for the hat and hat center templates. Trace or copy the other templates from the book, back them with sturdy cardboard, and then cut out of the cardboard. Use the templates to cut out the pieces listed below:
- 12 overalls from fabric scraps and 12 from fusible interfacing
- 12 shirts from fabric scraps and 12 from fusible interfacing
- 12 hats (large circle) from fabric scraps and 12 from fusible interfacing
- 12 hat centers (small circle) from fabric scraps and 12 from fusible interfacing
- Twelve 12-inch squares of Fabric A
- Six 3 × 45 inch strips of Fabric B (for joiner strips)
- Six 4 × 45 inch strips of Fabric B (for the inner border)
- Six 5 × 45 inch strips of Fabric C (for the outer border)
- Backing: cut into two lengths of 2 yards each and seam them together on a long side to make a pieced backing of 90 × 72 inches
- Binding: cut 4-inch-wide strips for single-thickness binding or 6-inch-wide strips for double-thickness binding

DIRECTIONS

All construction is done with right sides of fabric facing and ¼-inch seam allowances. Template patterns include ⅛-inch seam allowances, which will be used when

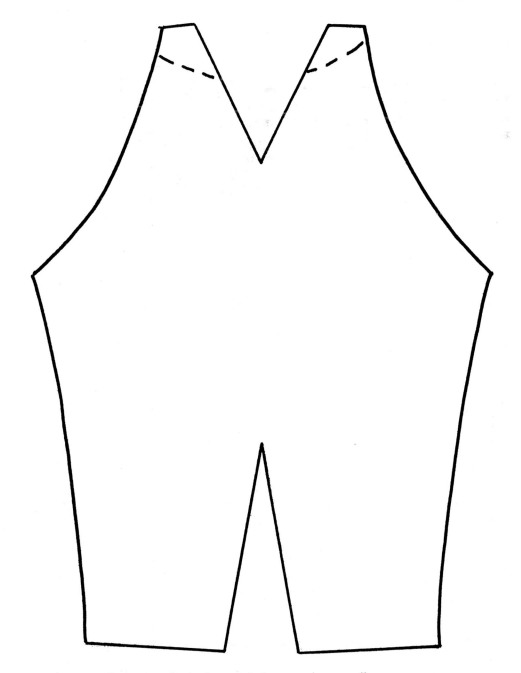

Full-size overall template; includes ¼-inch seam allowances.

we sew the appliqué pieces to the fusible interfacing. If you need a ¼-inch seam allowance for templates, add ⅛ inch around each.

1. Read the speed appliqué section in the "Speed Techniques" chapter and follow the directions to sew all the appliqué pieces to the interfacing. They should

Overall Bill

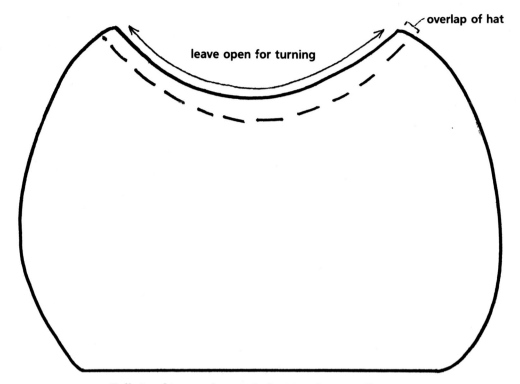

Full-size shirt template; includes ¼-inch seam allowances.

end up with the adhesive side out when you are finished. Fold each 12-inch square in half vertically and press; use the crease as the center line for positioning Overall Bill. Lay out an overalls, shirt, hat, and hat center on the 12-inch square. Position the shirt underneath, the overalls over that, the hat third, and the hat center on top. The topmost part of the hat should be about 1½ inches down from the top edge of the square. Press the positioned pieces in place with the iron on a low setting to avoid scorching the fabric. (Follow the directions for your particular kind of interfacing.) Once the appliqués are fused in place on the square, machine appliqué them in place. Attach and sew the appliqués to all 12 blocks in the same way.

2. Lay out your blocks in an arrangement that is pleasing to you, in four rows of three blocks across (see 13-1). Set blocks #3, #6, #9, and #12 aside for now (see illu. 13-1 for block numbering). Place a 3-inch wide Fabric B strip face up on the sewing machine bed. Lay the top right block (block #1) face down over it, with Overall Bill standing upright (see illu. 13-2); align the two pieces at the top and right, and stitch them together at the right, using a ¼ inch seam allowance here (and from this point on). Continue to add blocks to 3-inch-wide Fabric B strips until all the eight blocks (#1, #2, #4, #5, #7, #8, #10, and #11) are attached to a strip. (Take new B strips as needed.) Cut across the strip to separate the units (illu. 13-2). Now each of the eight blocks has a joiner strip at its left.

3. Sew the blocks with strips together in pairs: #1 and #2, #4 and #5, #7 and #8, and #10 and #11, as shown in illu. 13-3, to make a row of two blocks.

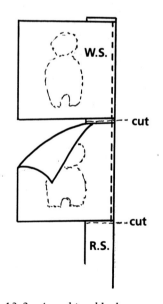

13-2. Attaching blocks to a joiner strip.

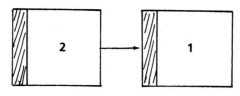

13-3. *Joining pairs of blocks.*

13-4. *Joining three blocks to make a row.*

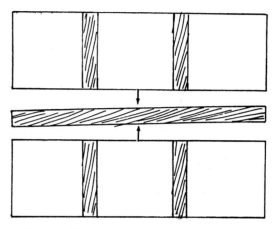

13-5. *Adding a joiner strip between rows.*

4. Place block #3 (from those you set aside earlier) face up on your sewing machine bed. Lay the two-block row of block #1 + #2 face down over it, making sure the joiner strip is at the right (see illu. 13-4). Overall Bill should be standing in the upright position on all. Stitch them together at the right to complete the first row of three blocks. Repeat this, attaching the remaining two-block rows to the remaining blocks (#6, #9, and #12) to complete all four rows.

5. Sew a 3-inch-wide Fabric B joiner strip in between two adjacent rows of blocks (13-5), so when you are done, the quilt center will look like the center in illus. 13-1. Trim the strips so they don't extend beyond the width of the row.

6. In the chapter on "Speed Techniques," read about adding borders. Take your six 4 × 45-inch inner border (Fabric B) strips. Sew one to the top and one to the bottom of the quilt center made in Step 5. Trim any extra border that extends beyond the quilt center width. Join two 4 × 45-inch Fabric B strips on a short side to each other, and use that for the side border of your quilt center. Trim off any excess. Make the second side border the same way (see 13-1).

7. Piece together the outer border strips on a short side and sew on the outer border in the same way as you did the first border. Finish the quilt as you like.

14. Twisted Log Cabin

Quilting in our day has become more than a way of keeping the family warm. It has become an artistic avenue of expression. Quilts years ago were stored by being laid 12 deep, or better, on a guest bed until the bed was needed. Today they are hung on walls, used for tablecloths, and placed wherever their beauty can be enjoyed. Marvelous patchwork is worn simply because of its excellence.

We have a love affair with quilts due to their versatility. They are beautiful; their historical value is not to be overlooked. They're an art form and those who make them are artists in the true sense of the word. Quilts have been a necessity in hard times to keep our families warm, or to help raise money. They have bridged generations. They have been like friends. When you make a quilt you feel generations melt away. You're doing what someone did possibly hundreds of years ago, and just for a short time that person is alive in your appreciation for her skill and artistry.

The pattern that follows brings us up to date. I chose it because it says a lot about our taste and the taste of our forefathers. The Log Cabin is one of the oldest North American patchwork patterns, yet it is still just as beloved as it ever was. We're always trying to find new ways to use it. We create pictures with the blocks or visual effects that are hard to achieve with any other pattern. The Twisted Log Cabin has a nice country look and feel while still saying, "I'm modern and I'm comfortable," satisfying even the most picky of quilters. The pattern given here is made up of 140 blocks (14 rows of 10 blocks each). Finished size: 67 × 87 inches. Block size: 5 × 5 inches. Approximate time to complete the quilt top: 12 hours; fairly easy, but watch the placement of the blocks.

YARDAGE*

- ⅓ yard of Fabric A (orange pink)
- ⅔ yard of Fabric B (black)
- ⅓ yard of Fabric C (green print)
- 1 yard of Fabric D (brown print)
- ⅔ yard of Fabric E (dark green solid)
- ⅔ yard of Fabric F (light green)
- 1 yard of Fabric G (pink with flowers)
- ⅔ yard of Fabric H (yellow)
- 1 yard of Fabric I (white)
- 1 yard of Fabric J for the first border (floral with dark green background)
- 1¼ yards of Fabric E for the second border (dark green)
- 1 yard of fabric to cut single-thickness bias binding or 1½ yards to cut double-thickness bias binding (light green)
- 5 yards of fabric for the backing
- 5 yards of batting (45 inches wide) or equivalent

*Colors in parentheses are the colors used in the model. Use whatever colors are pleasing to you, but keep their light and dark values the same to preserve the pattern.

Twisted Log Cabin

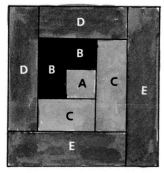

14-1. Block 1 (make 44).

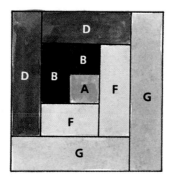

14-2. Block 2 (make 27).

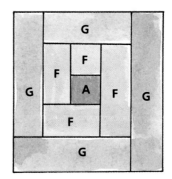

14-3. Block 3 (make 12).

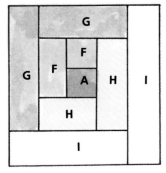

14-4. Block 4 (make 24).

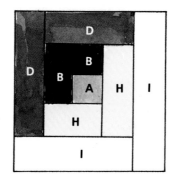

14-5. Block 5 (make 21).

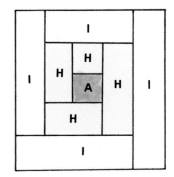

14-6. Block 6 (make 12).

CUTTING

All the strips listed below are the same size: 1½ × 45 inches

- 7 strips of Fabric A
- 11 strips of Fabric B
- 7 strips of Fabric C
- 20 strips of Fabric D
- 12 strips of Fabric E
- 14 strips of Fabric F
- 19 strips of Fabric G
- 14 strips of Fabric H
- 21 strips of Fabric I
- For the inner border, eight 4 × 45 inch strips of Fabric J
- For the outer border, eight 5 × 45 inch strips of Fabric E
- Backing: cut into two 2½-yard lengths and sew together on a long side to make a 90-inch square backing.

DIRECTIONS

Making the Blocks

This quilt may look hard to make, but it isn't; just use the worksheet given here so you can easily keep track of the fabrics, and it will go smoothly. The pattern is made with 6 different blocks (Block 1 through Block 6). Take a few minutes to look at illus. 14-1 through 14-6, so you have an idea of the layout of each block. Photocopy the worksheet given here six times (once for each block), or make your own, and use them as an assembly and fabric guide for each block. Tape the worksheet to your sewing machine or any convenient spot so you can see it while you're working. Each block grows like a snail from the inside out as you add strips.

In the body of the directions below, I tell you how to construct Block 1, but in parentheses, in numerical order, I give the amounts of times to cut something or the fabrics for the remaining five blocks. For example, "lay down a Fabric B strip (B, F, F, B, H)" means that for Block 1 you use a B strip, for Block 2 you use a B strip, for Block 3 you use an F strip, for Block 4 you use an F strip, for block 5 you use a B strip, and for Block 6 you use an H strip in this step. You will need to go through Steps 1 through 8 six times, once for each block type you are making, choosing the correct fabrics and instructions as you go along. By following the instructions you will make the number of blocks listed below:

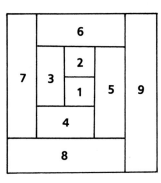

Order of growth of blocks.

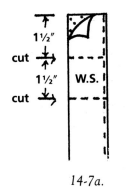

14-7a.

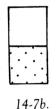

14-7b.

Block Type	How Many to Make
Block 1	44
Block 2	27
Block 3	12
Block 4	24
Block 5	21
Block 6	12

All construction is done with right sides of fabric facing and ¼-inch seam allowances.

1. Place a Fabric A (A, A, A, A, A) strip face up on your sewing machine, with a short end towards you. Lay a Fabric B (B, F, F, B, H) strip face down over it, and sew them together on one long side. Repeat 1 (0, 0, 0, 0, 0) time. Measure down from the top 1½ inches and cut across both strips (illu. 14-7a) to form a two-square block center (14-7b). You will need to cut a total of 44 (27, 12, 24, 21, 12) of these two-square block centers for this block.

2. Set a Fabric B (B, F, F, B, H) strip face up on your sewing machine bed. Top it with a two-square block center from Step 1, face down, being sure that the Fabric B (B, F, F, B, H) strip is to the top, and sew them together at the right, butting in new 2-square block centers until they have all been added to a strip. (Take new strips of the same fabric, as needed.) Cut the units apart across the strip, as shown in illu. 14-8a. Press the 3-piece units open. They will look like 14-8b.

3. Place a Fabric C (F, F, H, H, H) strip face up on your sewing machine bed. Lay your sewn 3-piece unit from Step 2 face down over the strip, aligned at top and right, making sure that the Fabric B piece (B, F, F, B, H) is to the top (A is to the lower right), and stitch them together at the right, butting in new 3-piece units until all have been added to a Fabric C (F, F, H, H, H) strip. Take new strips as needed. Cut the units apart across the strip as shown in illu. 14-9a. Press open the 4-piece units (illu. 14-9b). Keep checking to see that you are making the right number of blocks (see the block chart given earlier). In one of my classes, one woman's block was mislaid under some other fabric and she didn't notice until she was ready to put her quilt together; then she had to go back and finish the one lone block; this can be irritating. We want quilting to be fun!

4. Set a Fabric C (F, F, H, H, H) strip face up on your sewing machine bed. Cover it with a 4-piece unit from Step 3, with raw edges of the unit and the strip aligned at the right and top, making sure that the Fabric C (F, F, H, H, H) piece is to the top (see illu. 14-10a). Stitch the 4-piece unit and the strip together at the right, butting in new units until they are all attached to a strip. (Take new strips of the same fabric as needed.) Cut across the strip to separate the 5-piece units; they will look like 14-10a. Press them open.

5. Now lay a Fabric D (D, G, G, D, I) strip face up on your sewing machine bed. Place a 5-piece unit from Step 4 face down, with the longest Fabric C (F, F, H, H, H) piece to the top (see illu. 14-11a). Align the unit and strip at the top and right. Stitch them together at the right. Attach more 5-piece units, taking new strips as needed, until the units are all attached to a strip. Cut across the strip to separate the units, and press the 6-piece units open. They will look like illu. 14-11b.

6. Place a Fabric D (D, G, G, D, I) strip face up on your sewing machine bed. Cover it with a 6-piece unit from Step 5, face down, aligned at the right, with the just-added Fabric D (D, G, G, D, I) piece at the top (illu. 14-12a). Stitch them together at the right, butting in new 6-piece units, and taking new strips until all

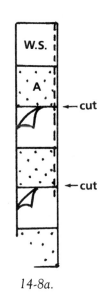

14-8a.

14-8b. A 3-piece unit.

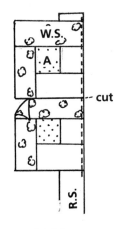

14-11a.

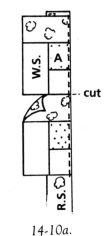

14-9a.

14-9b. A 4-piece unit.

14-10a.

14-10b. A 5-piece unit.

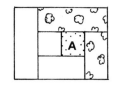

14-11b. A 6-piece unit.

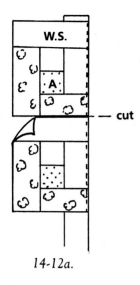

14-12a.

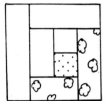

14-12b. A 7-piece unit.

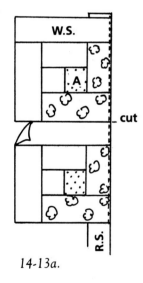

14-13a.

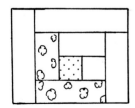

14-13b. An 8-piece unit.

the units are attached to a strip. Cut them apart across the strip and press the 7-piece units open; they will look like 14-12b.

7. Lay a Fabric E (G, G, I, I, I) strip face up on your sewing machine bed. Place a 7-piece unit over it, face down, aligned at the right and at the top, making sure the longest Fabric D piece (D, G, G, D, I) is at the top (illu. 14-13a). Stitch the unit and strip together at the right, butting in new units and taking new strips, until all the units are attached to strips of the same fabric. Cut across the strips to separate the 8-piece units, and press them open (14-13b).

8. Next, we'll add the last fabric strip to our blocks. Put a Fabric E (G, G, I, I, I) strip face up on your sewing machine bed. Top it with an 8-piece unit from Step 7, face down, aligned at right and at the top, making sure the just-joined Fabric E piece (G, G, I, I, I) is at the top. Stitch the strip to the unit at the right, adding in new 8-piece units and taking new strips, until all the units are attached to a strip. Cut across the strips to separate the units, and press them open. They are your finished blocks (whichever block you are working on); see 14-1 through 14-6 for the diagrams of the finished blocks.

Assembling the Blocks

Next, we need to assemble the blocks into rows, which will then be sewn together to make the quilt center. Lay out the blocks on a work surface and be sure that they are arranged correctly (refer to color photo if necessary). The Block Placement and Orientation Chart shows how the blocks should be laid out for each row. The dark L shape in each place in the chart shows how the darker side of the chart should be placed. (A box on the chart means all 4 sides of the block are the same color.) Make sure the blocks are in the correct order *and* turned correctly. You may want to tag the top of each block with a bit of masking tape to be sure its orientation doesn't get changed as you handle it.

9. Sew each block in the row to the next one, until you have joined all ten on the row. Repeat for the other 13 rows. After the blocks are sewn into rows, sew the rows together to form the center of the quilt top.

10. Following the directions under attaching borders in the "Speed Techniques" chapter, add the borders and finish the quilt as you like. Many Log Cabin quilts are tied, or quilted in a simple outline pattern.

Block Placement and Orientation Chart*

For rows 1 and 14	1	1	1	1	1	1	1	1	1	1
For rows 2, 6, and 10	1	2	4	6	5	5	6	4	2	1
For rows 3, 7, and 11	1	2	3	4	5	2	4	6	2	1
For rows 4, 8, and 12	1	5	4	3	2	2	3	4	5	1
For rows 5, 9, and 13	1	5	6	4	2	5	4	3	2	1

*Closed boxes □ mean that all sides are the same color.
└ indicates the position of the darker side of the block.

Worksheet for Twisted Log Cabin Blocks

Pin a swatch of fabric next to its letter below. Also glue a swatch of the correct fabric in place on the block diagram, as a guide in visualizing how your block will look and will be pieced. For each of the six blocks (Blocks 1 through 6) make a separate worksheet.

Fabric A:

Fabric B:

Fabric C:

Fabric D:

Fabric E:

Fabric F:

Fabric G:

Fabric H:

Fabric I:

Block: _____

15. Amish Diamond in Square

Amish settlers, members of an offshoot of the Mennonite religion, came from Switzerland to Pennsylvania beginning in the 1720s, seeking religious freedom. They are a quiet and gentle people; this is reflected in their quilts. When you look at their quilts, you get a feeling for the simple life that they lead and the love of peace and harmony that they hold so dear. Although their quilts were made for use and not only for decoration, they are works of art, with bold colors, strong geometric shapes, and beautiful textures resulting from rich quilting, which is well placed in the large areas of solid colors (patterned fabrics aren't used).

In the Amish Diamond given here, the large center diamond has an inside border, called a "fence," used to fence in the main design (see illu. 15-1). The same sense of order and neatness you'll see in the wonderful Amish farms is found in the quilts. Approximate time to complete the quilt top, 4 hours; very easy. Quilt size: 96 × 96 inches.

YARDAGE*

- 1 yard of Fabric A (red)
- 2½ yards of Fabric B (purplish blue, for inner borders)
- 1¼ yards of Fabric C (magenta)
- 4½ yards of Fabric D (dark blue; for outer border)
- 6 yards of batting (45 inches wide) or equivalent
- 6 yards of fabric for backing
- 1¼ yards of fabric to cut single-thickness binding or 1¾ yards of fabric to cut double-thickness binding

*Colors in parentheses are the colors in the model. Use whatever colors are pleasing to you.

CUTTING

- 30-inch square of Fabric A
- Four 4 × 45 inch strips of Fabric B
- Eight 5½ × 45 inch strips of Fabric B
- Eight 18 × 45 inch strips of Fabric D
- Backing: cut fabric into two 3-yard lengths and seam together on a long side to make a 90 × 108 inch pieced backing
- Binding: for single-thickness binding cut 4-inch-wide strips; for double-thickness binding cut 6-inch-wide strips.

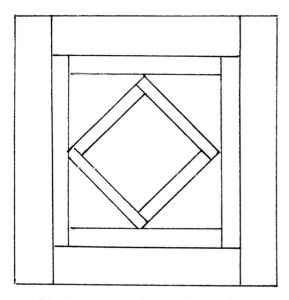

15-1. Construction diagram for Amish Diamond in Square.

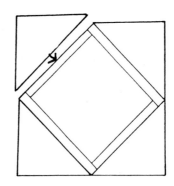

15-2. Attaching the inside border.

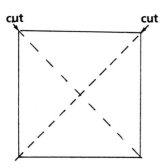

15-3. Making triangles.

15-4. Attaching the triangles.

DIRECTIONS

All construction is done with right sides of fabric facing and ¼-inch seam allowances.

1. Read the section in the "Speed Techniques" chapter about adding borders. Working with your 30-inch Fabric A square, "fence it in" (add the inside border) by cutting and sewing on four of the 4-inch-wide Fabric B strips (15-2). Cut two to the length of two opposite sides of the square, and sew them on. Cut two more, to the length of the square plus the width of the side borders, and sew them on.

2. Measure the outside of the pieced unit you just made. It is probably around 35 inches. Whatever the length, cut a Fabric C square whose side is also that length; for example, if the side of the pieced unit is 35.5 inches, cut a 35.5 inch square of Fabric C. Cut the Fabric C square in half on the diagonal, and cut on the other diagonal to make 4 triangles (illu. 15-3). Sew one triangle on its long side to each side of the fenced square (illu. 15-4).

Amish Diamond in Square

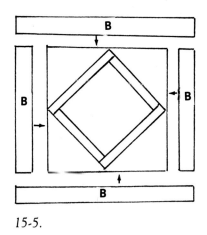

15-5.

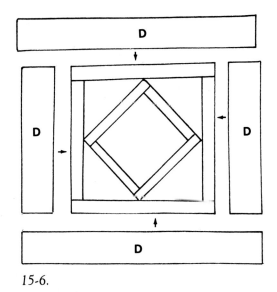

15-6.

3. Now let's add a border around the square we created in Step 2, using the 5½-inch-wide Fabric B strips (15-5). Piece two of the strips together on their short sides. Piece two more the same way. Sew the strips to 2 opposite sides of the square and trim off the excess. Continue piecing 5½-inch-wide B strips and sew them to the top and bottom of the square for top and bottom borders, as needed; trim off the excess.

4. Piece two 18-inch-wide Fabric D strips on a long side. Repeat to make 4 pairs. Add on the last border, using the 18-inch-wide strips, in the same way as we added the previous border (illu. 15-6).

5. With the Amish Diamond in Square, there is a great deal of open space that can be filled with hand quilting. If this is not your specialty, try machine quilting or even tying the quilt with different colors of thread, to form a pattern. Whatever you choose, have fun and enjoy your work of art.

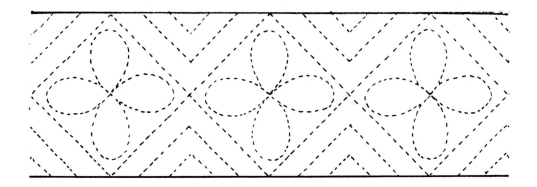

16. Sunbonnet Sue

Sunbonnet Sue was one of the quilts that was very popular from the 1920s through the 1940s. Starting in the mid-1800s, patterns with little girls began to show up. Because she was easier to change than her counterpart, Overall Bill, Sunbonnet Sue became very popular. As the years went by, her clothes were updated, so she was loved by young and old alike. Approximate time to complete the quilt top, 9 hours; fairly easy. Finished size: 56 × 69.5 inches. Finished block size (not including seam allowances) 11½ × 11½ inches. If you wish this quilt to be larger, add more blocks or more borders. This is a great pattern for using up those small, favorite pieces of fabric you have on hand.

YARDAGE*

- ¼ yard of Fabric A (for sleeves; patterned in model)
- ¼ yard of Fabric B (flesh-colored)
- About 1¼ yards of assorted print and solid fabric scraps for appliqués
- 1½ yards of Fabric C (white)
- 1¼ yards of Fabric D for joiner strips and inner border (black print with flowers)
- 1 yard of Fabric E for outer border (pink)
- 4 yards of fabric for backing
- 4 yards of batting (45 inches wide) or equivalent
- 1 yard of fusible interfacing (45 inches) or equivalent
- 1 yard of fabric for cutting single-thickness bias binding or 1¾ yards of fabric for cutting double-thickness bias binding
- ¾ yard fabric to cut single-thickness bias binding or 1¼ yard to cut double thickness

*Colors in parentheses are the colors in the model. Use whatever colors are pleasing to you.

CUTTING

- 3 × 45 inch strip of Fabric A
- 1½ × 45 inch strip of Fabric B
- Twelve 12-inch squares of Fabric C
- Six 3 × 45-inch joiner strips of Fabric D
- Six 4 × 45 inch strips of Fabric D (for inner border)
- Six 5 × 45 inch strips of Fabric E (for outer border)
- Backing: cut the fabric into two 72-inch lengths and sew them on a long side to make a 90 × 72 inch pieced backing.
- Binding: Cut strips 4 inches wide for single-thickness bias binding or 6 inches wide for double-thickness.

Sunbonnet Sue

113

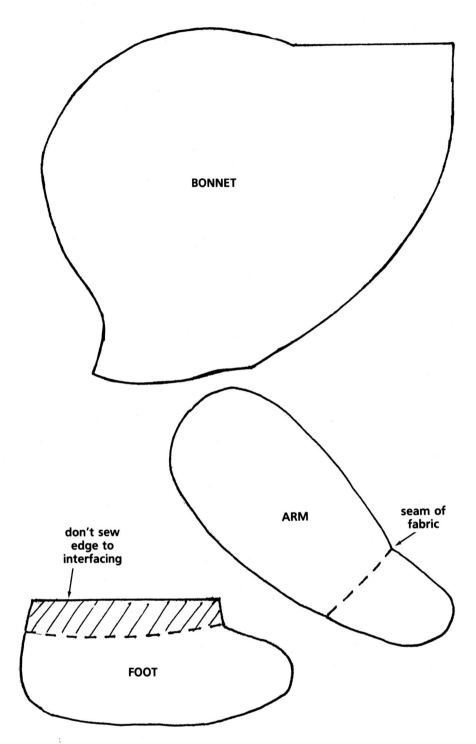

Full-size hat, arm, and foot templates; ⅛-inch seam allowances are included. Shaded area of foot should be placed under the skirt appliqué before fusing.

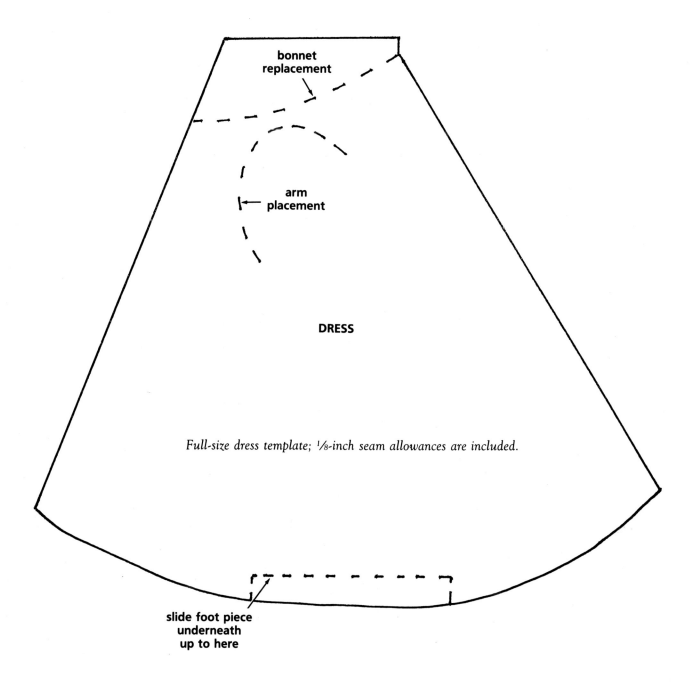

bonnet replacement

arm placement

DRESS

Full-size dress template; ⅛-inch seam allowances are included.

slide foot piece underneath up to here

DIRECTIONS

All construction is done with right sides of fabric facing and ¼ inch seam allowances. See "Speed Techniques" chapter regarding speed appliqué. When sewing Sunbonnet Sue pieces to the interfacing, we will be using ⅛-inch seam allowances. The appliqué templates have ⅛-inch seam allowances built in. If you need ¼ inch, add ⅛ inch more around each template.

1. Trace out the dress, arm, hat, and foot templates, cut them out of the paper, and back them on stiff cardboard.

2. Place the 3-inch-wide Fabric A strip (for the sleeves) face up. Lay the 1½-inch-wide Fabric B strip (for the hands) face down over it. Sew them together along one long side. Press the fabrics open. Using the arm template provided, cut out 12 arms. The hand should be on the flesh-colored fabric (Fabric B), with the seamline on the template on the seamline between the strips.

3. Read the directions for speed appliqué in the "Speed Techniques" chapter. Make sure that all patterns are face up when you cut, and cut on the front of the fabric, otherwise some of the pieces will be reversed. Cut out 12 of each from the fabric scraps: hats, dresses, and feet, using the templates. Cut 12 of each template shape from interfacing also. Follow the directions in the "Speed Techniques" chapter to sew an interfacing piece onto all appliqué pieces; be sure that they will end up with the adhesive side of the interfacing on the outside when finished. Note that the top edge of the foot piece is not sewn to the interfacing, but is left open.

4. On a 12-inch square of Fabric C, lay out a dress with a foot under it and a bonnet and arm over, as shown on the dress template, using the photo as a guide. Fuse the pieces in place with an iron on a low setting to avoid scorching the fabric, and follow the specific instructions given with the interfacing you use for pressing. Once the pieces are fused in place, machine appliqué them in place. Read the speed appliqué instructions in the "Speed Techniques" chapter for further information. Complete the other 11 appliqué blocks in the same way.

5. Lay out the blocks in four rows of 3 blocks each on your work surface, in an arrangement that is pleasing to you. Number each with a bit of tape to keep track of the order (see illu. 16-1). Set aside blocks #3, #6, #9, and #12. Place a Fabric D joiner strip (3 × 45 inches) face up on the sewing machine bed. Lay one

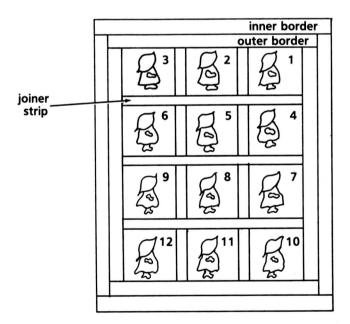

16-1. Construction diagram for Sunbonnet Sue.

of the remaining blocks face down over it, with edges aligned at top and right. Sunbonnet Sue should be with the head at the top, as shown in illu. 16-2a. Stitch the block to the strip at the right, with ¼ inch seam allowance. Continue to sew blocks to the strip; about 4 will fit. Take another joiner strip and attach another 4; then cut them apart across the strip to separate the units, and press them open. You will now have eight blocks with short joiner strips at the left (see 16-2b).

6. Sew the Block 1 + joiner strip unit to the Block 2 + joiner strip unit (see illu. 16-3). Add Block 3 (see 16-3). This completes the first row of blocks. Complete the other three rows of blocks in the same way, and press them.

7. Sew a Fabric D joiner strip (3 × 45 inches) between row 1 and row 2, between row 2 and row 3, between row 3 and row 4 to complete the quilt center (see 16-1 for reference). Trim off any excess of strip that extends beyond the blocks.

8. Read the section about adding borders in the "Speed Techniques" chapter. Sew the two inner border (4-inch-wide Fabric D) strips together on a short side, and sew that to the side of the quilt center as the side inner border. Trim off the excess, and sew another inner border strip to the opposite side of the quilt center. Sew the top and bottom inner border strips to the quilt center in the same way, except they extend to include the width of the side borders. Trim off the excess border.

9. Sew together the 45-inch lengths of the outer border strips (Fabric E) on a short side to make long strips; attach them to the unit made in Step 8 to make the outer border, as you did for the inner border.

10. Finish the quilt as you wish.

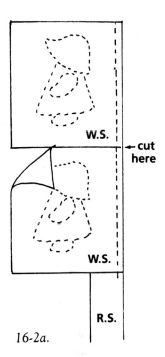

W.S.

← cut here

W.S.

R.S.

16-2a.

16-3.

16-2b.

17. Basket Quilt

Basket and flowerpot patterns have been popular since the early 19th century. Basket patterns were more popular, because they were beautiful with or without flowers. Empty-basket quilts can be found all over the country. As a general rule, the basket block is alternated with a plain block, which is quilted with a feathered circle pattern. Sometimes the handles play an important part of the overall pattern.

The quilt center consists of nine pieced blocks and four solid blocks, set on point, surrounded by triangles (see illu. 17-1). Approximate time to complete the quilt top, 10 to 12 hours; fairly easy. Finished size: 71 × 71 inches. Finished block size (without seam allowances): 12 inches × 12 inches.

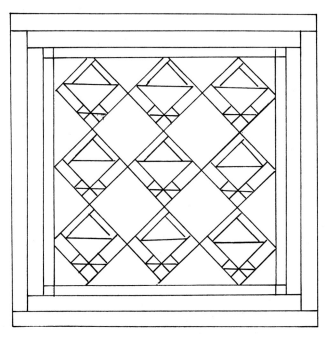

17-1. Construction diagram for Basket Quilt.

YARDAGE*

- 2 yards of Fabric A (white)
- 1¼ yards of Fabric B (blue print)
- ¼ yard of Fabric C (white floral print)
- ¾ yard of Fabric D for the first border (tan print)
- 1 yard of Fabric E for the second border (red-white-blue print)
- 1½ yards of Fabric F for the third border (blue print)
- 4 yards of fabric for the backing
- 4 yards of batting (45 inches wide) or equivalent
- For binding: 1 yard of fabric to cut single-thickness binding or 1½ yards of fabric to cut double-thickness binding

*Colors in parentheses are the colors in the model. Use whatever colors are pleasing to you.

118

CUTTING

- 10 × 45 inch strip of Fabric A
- Two 6½ × 45 inch strips of Fabric A
- 3½ × 45 inch strip of Fabric A
- Nine 12½-inch squares of Fabric A: cut 4 on one diagonal to make large triangles; also cut one on both diagonals to quarter the square and make small triangles
- 10 × 45 inch strip of Fabric B
- Five 2 × 45 inch strips of Fabric B
- Five 9½-inch squares of Fabric B: cut each one on a diagonal, for the bottoms of the baskets
- Five 6½-inch squares of Fabric C: cut on one diagonal, for the insides of the baskets
- Eight 3 × 45 inch strips of Fabric D for the first border
- Eight 4 × 45 inch strips of Fabric E for the second border
- Eight 5 × 45 inch strips of Fabric F for the third border
- Binding: 4 inches wide for single-thickness binding; 6 inches wide for double-thickness binding

DIRECTIONS

All construction is done with ¼-inch seam allowances and right sides of fabric facing.

1. Read the directions for triangle squares in the chapter on "Speed Techniques." Take your 10-inch strips of Fabric A and Fabric B. Using the directions, graph out ten 4-inch squares on the wrong side of the lighter fabric, and mark the diagonals (illu. 17-2). Pin both fabrics together face to face, and sew ¼ inch away from the diagonals on either side of them. Cut along the diagonal lines and square lines, and press the units open to get 20 triangle squares. (You only need 18 for the quilt. If you use all 20, you will have an extra basket, and can choose the best nine for the quilt top. You could use the extra basket for a pillow or a square in a sampler quilt.) Press the triangle squares and set them aside.

2. Place a 2 × 45 inch Fabric B strip face up on your sewing machine bed. Lay a Fabric C triangle, cut from a 6½ inch square face down as shown in illu.

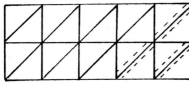

17-2a.

17-2b.

Basket Quilt

17-3, over the strip so that the short side of the triangle aligns with the edge of the strip. Stitch them together as shown in illu. 17-3. Lay another triangle of Fabric C face down over the strip, 2 inches below the end of the last one, and stitch them together at the right. Repeat to attach the remaining Fabric C triangles—about 5 will fit on a strip. Take another Fabric B strip to attach the rest of them. Cut the units apart across the strip, as shown in illu. 17-3.

3. Lay a 2 × 45 inch Fabric B strip face up on your sewing machine bed. Place a unit from Step 2 face down over it, with the 6½ inch triangle positioned as shown in illus. 17-4. Stitch the triangle to the strip at the right. Position another unit from Step 2 two inches further down on the strip, and stitch it in the same way as the first one. Continue adding the units from Step 2 to the B strips, taking another B strip when it is needed. After all the units are attached to strips, cut them apart across the strip as shown in illus. 17-4. Press the units open and trim the edges of the strips at an angle, as shown in illus. 17-5. These are the basket tops.

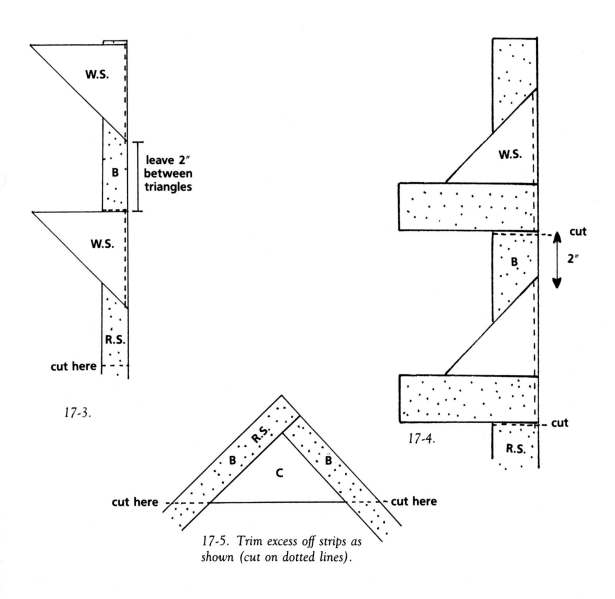

17-3.

17-4.

17-5. *Trim excess off strips as shown (cut on dotted lines).*

4. Place a Fabric B triangle, cut from a 10-inch square, face up, and cover it with a basket top from Step 3, face down, aligned so that the long sides of the triangles are aligned at the right (illu. 17-6a). Stitch them together on the long side. Press the unit open. Repeat this with the remaining nine basket tops and Fabric B triangles. The basket will look like illu. 17-6b. Set them aside.

5. Put a 6½ inch Fabric A strip face up on your sewing machine bed. Top it with one of the triangle squares you made in Step 1, face down. Position it as shown in illu. 17-7. Butt in triangle squares below it, and sew them to the strip at the right until all 10 have been added. Cut them apart across the strips, as shown in illu. 17-7. Then take a good look at illu. 17-8. Sew the strip plus triangle square unit to the bottom of the basket (from Step 4), as shown in illu. 17-8, with right sides of fabric facing and ¼-inch seam allowances, as usual. Join the remaining nine triangle units to the ten baskets in the same way.

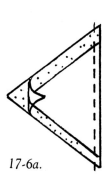

17-6a.

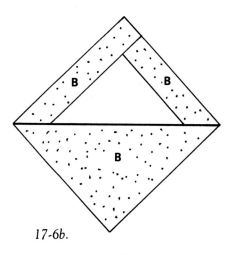

17-6b.

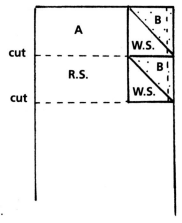

17-7.

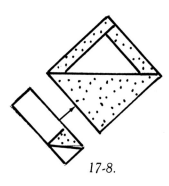

17-8.

6. Place a 3½ × 45 inch strip of Fabric A face up on your sewing machine bed. Top it with a triangle square from Step 1, positioned as shown in illu. 17-9a, face down, aligned with the strip at the top and the right. Stitch them together at the right. Join 9 more triangle squares to the A strip in the same way. Cut the units apart across the strip and press them open. They will look like illu. 17-9b.

7. Lay a 6½ × 45 inch Fabric A strip face up on your sewing machine bed. Place a pieced unit from Step 6 over it, wrong side up, as shown in illu. 17-10a. Sew them together at the right, and continue adding all ten pieced units in the same way. Cut them apart across the strip. The finished units will look like 17-10b. Press them open. These are the pieced strips for the lower right edge of the basket. Sew each to a basket, as shown in illu. 17-11.

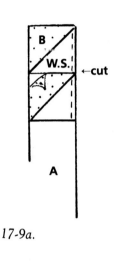

17-9a.

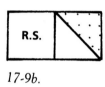

17-9b.

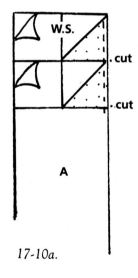

17-10a.

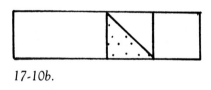

17-10b.

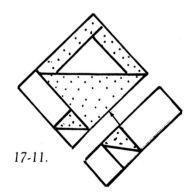

17-11.

8. To assemble the quilt center, first look at illu. 17-12. The blocks are set on point in 2 corner units and 3 rows. All the triangles and solid blocks are of Fabric A. All the large triangles are sewn on a short side.

Corner Unit 1: Sew a small triangle on its long side to the top left side of a pieced block; sew a large triangle to the right and left sides of the pieced block (see illu. 17-12 for reference). Set the unit aside.

Row 1: Sew the units together in the order: large triangle + pieced block + solid block + pieced block + large triangle. See illu. 17-12 for details.

Row 2: Sew the units together in the order: small triangle + pieced block + solid block + pieced block + solid block + pieced block + small triangle (the small triangles are sewn on their long side or hypotenuse).

Row 3: large triangle + pieced block + solid block + pieced block + large triangle.

Corner Unit 2: Sew a small triangle to the lower right side of a pieced block. Sew a large triangle to the block's lower left and upper right sides.

9. Once the corner units and rows are made, sew them together to form the quilt center (see illu. 17-12 for reference).

10. To finish the quilt, read about adding borders in the "Speed Techniques" chapter. Add the inner, middle, and outer borders, piecing border strips as needed. Finish the quilt as you like. The large solid blocks and triangles are perfect places for beautiful quilting patterns.

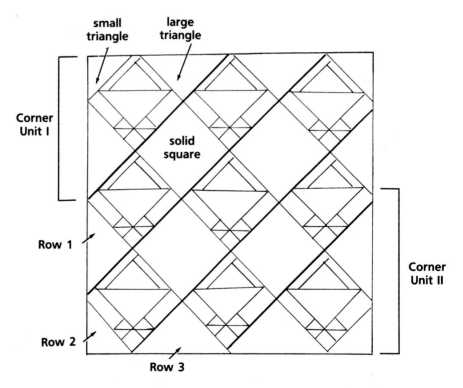

17-12. Diagram showing corner units and rows (divided by heavy lines).